Money Mindset and Math:
Unlocking Financial Freedom Through Mindset and Action

Shubham Saxena

Copyright

Copyright © Shubham Saxena, 2023 All rights reserved. No part of this publication may be reproduced, distributed, or transmitted in any form or by any means, including photocopying, recording, or other electronic or mechanical methods, without the prior written permission of the publisher, except in the case of brief quotations embodied in critical reviews and certain other noncommercial uses permitted by copyright law. For permission requests, please contact the author at joinengineeringwealth@gmail.com or visit https://www.facebook.com/joinengineeringwealth

First Edition: 2023

Reservation of Rights: The author reserves all rights to this book, including but not limited to the right to reproduce and distribute copies of the book.

Disclaimer: The advice and strategies found within may not be suitable for every situation. This work is sold with the understanding that neither the author nor the publisher are held responsible for the results accrued from the advice in this book.

Acknowledgement

"I would like to begin by expressing my deepest gratitude to my parents, whose love and support have been the foundation of my life. Their unwavering belief in me has been a constant source of inspiration and motivation.

I am also grateful to my friends, who have been my sounding board, my confidants, and my source of laughter and joy. Your support and encouragement has been invaluable to me throughout the writing of this book.

I would also like to extend my heartfelt thanks to my teachers and gurus, who have imparted their wisdom and knowledge and guided me on my journey. Their teachings have been instrumental in shaping my thoughts and ideas.

Finally, I would like to thank technology for providing me with the tools and resources to bring this book to fruition.

Thank you all for being a part of my journey and for your invaluable contributions to this book."

Money Mindset and Math: Unlocking Financial Freedom through Mindset and Action

Contents

PART-1: 7

Achieving Financial Freedom Through Mindset 7

Chapter 1 8

Introduction 8

   Understanding Financial Literacy 8

   Understanding Financial Freedom 10

   Financial Security vs Financial Freedom 12

Chapter 2 15

The Role of Emotions in Financial Decision-Making 15

   The Influence of Upbringing and Society on Money Attitudes ... 17

   The Role of Education System in Shaping Money Attitudes 19

   Cognitive Biases: Over Confidence and Sunk Cost Fallacy 23

Chapter 3 25

Building Mindset for Wealth Creation 25

   Growth vs Scarcity Mindset 25

   The Importance of Financial Planning 27

   The Importance of Budgeting and Money Management 29

   Shifting from Saving Mindset to Investing Mindset 31

Chapter 4 37

Understanding Key Financial Concepts 37

Assets and liabilities 37

Active Income vs Passive Income 39

Understanding Personal Income Statement: 42

Comparing Income Statements of Poor, Middle-Class and Rich 42

The Time Value of Money 46

Chapter 5 48

The Power of Compounding 48

Introduction 48

Compounding: The Greatest Discovery in Mathematics of All Time 50

Chapter 6 55

Warren Buffet's Journey to the Top 55

The First Million Dollars 57

The Snowball Effect 58

Key Takeaways from Warren Buffet's Investment Style 60

PART 2: 66

Achieving Financial Freedom Through Action 66

Chapter 7 67

Learning to do the Math: The First Step Towards Accumulating Wealth 67

Introduction 67

Using Excel for Financial Calculations 69

Retirement planning *91*

Chapter 8 .... **94**

The Wealth Creation Hut **94**

Introduction *94*

Active Income *101*

Portfolio Building *109*

Passive Income *111*

Second Income *117*

Chapter 9 .... **120**

Investment in Stock Market **120**

Long Term Investing Vs Short Term Speculation *123*

Direct Stock Investments *145*

Investment Philosophies *164*

Chapter 10 .... **173**

Diversifying Portfolio with Alternative Investments **173**

Debt vs Equity *173*

Investment in Debt Instruments *174*

Alternative Investments *182*

Portfolio Allocation *190*

What Not to Do as a Long-Term Investor *192*

Conclusion **200**

PART-1:

Achieving Financial Freedom Through Mindset

Chapter 1

Introduction

The quote, "If you took all the money and divide it equally among everybody, it would soon be back in the same pockets as it was before," is a powerful reminder of the dynamic nature of wealth and its accumulation. The statement suggests that even if wealth were to be distributed evenly among the population, it would eventually find its way back into the hands of a select few individuals. This is because the accumulation of wealth is not solely determined by one's income, but rather by one's mindset and approach towards money.

Understanding Financial Literacy

Financial literacy, or the ability to understand and manage one's finances, plays a crucial role in the accumulation of wealth. Education and professional expertise alone do not guarantee financial literacy. One may possess a high level of education and professional expertise, but still lack the necessary knowledge and understanding of financial concepts to effectively manage and grow their wealth. On the other hand, individuals who possess a sense of financial literacy, regardless of their level of education, possess the knowledge and understanding to accumulate and preserve wealth effectively. It is a common observation that some individuals, despite earning a substantial income, are unable to accumulate wealth, while others with a strong financial acumen are able to achieve financial freedom. This disparity highlights the importance of financial literacy in the pursuit of wealth and financial stability.

In this book, we will delve into the concepts of financial literacy and the mindset that drives financial success. We will explore various strategies and techniques to improve financial literacy and help individuals achieve financial freedom. We will examine the importance of budgeting, saving, investing, and managing debt in the accumulation of wealth. We will also explore the psychological and behavioral aspects of money management and how they impact one's ability to accumulate wealth. We will also discuss the importance of setting financial goals and developing a plan to achieve them. We will examine the different types of investment opportunities and the benefits and risks associated with each. We will also discuss the importance of diversifying one's portfolio and the role of professional financial advisors in the accumulation of wealth.

Whether you are just starting out on your financial journey or are looking to take your wealth-building efforts to the next level, this book is designed to provide valuable insights and practical advice to help you achieve your financial goals. With the knowledge and understanding gained from this book, you will be equipped with the tools and mindset necessary to accumulate and preserve wealth effectively.

Understanding Financial Freedom

Financial freedom is not just about being able to pay your bills and having a roof over your head, it's about having the ability to do what you truly love without worrying about money. It's about having enough passive income streams that you don't have to rely on a 9-5 job to make ends meet. It's about having the freedom to make decisions based on what you truly want, rather than what you can afford. To achieve financial freedom, one must first understand the difference between active income and passive income. Active income is the income that you earn from working, whether it's from a job or self-employment. Passive income, on the other hand, is income that you earn without actively working for it. This includes income from investments, rental properties, and businesses that run on autopilot.

Many people fall into the trap of thinking that buying a house is a good investment. While a house can be a good investment in certain circumstances, it's important to understand that it's not a guaranteed path to financial freedom. When you take out a mortgage, you are essentially trading your future income for a roof over your head. You are also taking on a large amount of debt, which can limit your ability to invest in other opportunities that can generate passive income. The key to financial freedom is to diversify your income streams. This means investing in a variety of different assets that can generate passive income. It's important to invest in assets that have the potential to appreciate in value, such as stocks, real estate, and businesses. It's also important to invest in assets that generate regular income, such as bonds and dividend-paying stocks.

In the next chapter of this book, we will go into more detail about different types of passive income streams and how you can start building them. We will also discuss the importance of budgeting, saving and managing your money in a way that will help you achieve your financial goals. Remember, financial freedom is not something that can be achieved overnight, it takes time and effort, but with the right mindset and approach, it's possible to achieve the financial freedom you desire.

Financial Security vs Financial Freedom

To truly grasp the concept of financial freedom, we must first understand what it is not. Merely being financially secure does not necessarily mean that you have achieved financial freedom. However, attaining financial freedom does guarantee financial security. Our education system often conditions our minds to become fearful of losing money and when it comes to the subject of finances, we tend to stop thinking logically and start thinking emotionally.

One of the most common examples of this is when it comes to buying a house. Many people are sold the idea of homeownership by being promised "low down payments," "easy monthly EMIs," and "tax benefits." However, what they fail to realize is that a house can actually be a significant liability on your income statement unless you are able to finance it through the stream of income generated by your assets. The government also plays a role in this system, as it often lures citizens into buying a house by offering tax benefits. But it is important to understand that this is not truly a benefit. It is like a scheme where you are being offered "Give me a 100 rupee note and I will give you a 10 rupee note in return." It is important to understand that these tax benefits are not true benefits and it is not in your best interest to fall for them. In the next chapters of this book, we will delve deeper into understanding the difference between assets and liabilities and how to build a solid financial foundation through acquiring assets that generate income for you. We will also discuss how to avoid the trap of falling for the false promises of "tax benefits" and instead focus on building true financial freedom through smart investments.

Being financially secure is a great accomplishment, but it is not the same as achieving financial freedom. Financial security means that you have a steady source of income and enough savings to take care of your expenses, but it does not guarantee that you have the freedom to leave your job and still maintain your current lifestyle. To truly achieve financial freedom, you need to have multiple streams of income that are not dependent on your 9-to-5 job. This means investing in assets that generate passive income, such as rental properties, stocks, or business ventures.

Achieving financial freedom takes discipline and hard work, as it requires you to think differently and take calculated risks. It means being willing to learn new skills and take on new challenges, rather than being content with the status quo. It also means having the discipline to save and invest a significant portion of your income, rather than spending it all on luxury items or short-term pleasures. It is worth noting that, the government policies and schemes are not always supportive of achieving financial freedom, as they often provide incentives for people to take on debt and become dependent on their jobs for income. It's important to educate oneself about such schemes and policies, and make informed decisions about how to best utilize them for achieving financial independence.

In summary, achieving financial freedom requires a combination of hard work, discipline, and a willingness to think differently and take calculated risks. It is not an easy journey, but it is one that can bring true freedom and control over one's life and financial future.

Chapter 2

The Role of Emotions in Financial Decision-Making

Money is often seen as a simple exchange of value, a tool for buying goods and services that we need or want. However, the reality is that money can have a much more profound and far-reaching impact on our lives than we might initially realize. One of the most significant ways that money can affect us is through its emotional and psychological impact. Money can be a powerful source of stress and anxiety for many people. For example, those struggling to make ends meet may experience feelings of hopelessness, frustration, and even shame. On the other hand, those who have more than enough money may feel a sense of guilt or even emptiness. Money can also be a source of conflict within relationships, whether it's due to disagreements over spending habits or resentment over one partner's perceived financial shortcomings.

Money can also have a significant impact on our self-esteem and self-worth. People often tie their sense of worth and success to their financial status, and those who feel they are not doing well financially may feel like they have failed in some way. This can lead to feelings of insecurity and even depression. On the other hand, having money and financial security can give people a sense of confidence and control over their lives, which can have a positive impact on their overall well-being. It's also important to consider how money can impact us in terms of our identity and values. People often see money as a symbol of what they stand for, it can be a representation of their hard work and success, their generosity and caring for others, or their ability to live the life they want. These meanings that people associate with money can be very powerful and can shape the way they think and feel about money, as well as the way they use it.

Additionally, emotions like fear and greed can also play a big role in our financial behavior. Fear can cause us to make hasty, panicked decisions, such as selling all of our investments during a market downturn. On the other hand, greed can lead us to make impulsive, over-eager investment decisions, such as buying into a stock that is experiencing rapid growth, even though there are no fundamentals to support it. Emotions can also impact our financial behavior through the way they shape our beliefs and attitudes. For example, if we believe that money can buy happiness, we may find ourselves overspending on unnecessary luxury items, even if we can't afford them. Similarly, if we believe that being wealthy is a sign of success, we may feel pressure to maintain a certain lifestyle, even if it is not sustainable.

In conclusion, money can have a powerful emotional and psychological impact on people. It can be a source of stress and anxiety, conflict in relationships, and affect our self-esteem and self-worth. Additionally, it can also shape our identity and values. Understanding the emotional and psychological dimensions of money can help us to better manage our finances, as well as our overall well-being. It's important to be aware of the emotions and thoughts associated with money and to work on developing a healthy relationship with it.

The Influence of Upbringing and Society on Money Attitudes

Our attitudes towards money are shaped by a complex interplay of factors, including our upbringing and life experiences. Understanding how these factors influence our attitudes can help us to better manage our finances and improve our overall well-being. One of the most significant factors that shape our attitudes towards money is our upbringing. For example, if we were raised in a household where money was always tight and financial stress was a constant presence, we may develop a sense of scarcity and anxiety around money. On the other hand, if we were raised in a household where money was abundant and financial security was taken for granted, we may develop a sense of entitlement and a lack of appreciation for the value of money.

Additionally, our experiences and exposure to different financial situations and cultures can also shape our attitudes towards money. For example, if we have had experiences of financial hardship, we may develop a frugal attitude towards money and a strong desire for financial security. On the other hand, if we have had experiences of financial abundance and privilege, we may develop a more carefree attitude towards money and be less motivated to save and invest. It's also important to consider the impact of societal and cultural influences on our attitudes towards money. Societal norms and expectations can shape our beliefs and attitudes around money, such as the idea that money can buy happiness or that being wealthy is a sign of success. Furthermore, cultural background and cultural values can also influence the way we think and feel about money. For example, in some cultures, money is seen as a symbol of status and prestige, whereas in others it is seen as a tool for fulfilling obligations to family and community.

In conclusion, our attitudes towards money are shaped by a complex interplay of factors, including our upbringing, life experiences, societal and cultural influences. Understanding these factors can help us to better understand our own attitudes and behaviors towards money, and take steps to develop a healthier relationship with it. It's important to be aware of the impact of these factors and to be mindful of the beliefs and attitudes that we have about money, and to work on developing a healthy mindset towards it.

The Role of Education System in Shaping Money Attitudes

As you may already know, financial literacy is essential for achieving financial success. However, it's unfortunate that our traditional education system often doesn't place enough emphasis on this important topic. Sure, we learn math and other subjects, but we're not always taught how to apply that knowledge to our financial lives. This can make it difficult for many people to set and achieve financial goals, and it can also make it harder for us to contribute to the economic growth of our country. One of the ways that we can contribute to the economic growth of our country is by investing our money. When we invest our money, we're essentially putting it to work for us. This can include things like depositing money in a bank, buying stocks or bonds, or even investing in real estate. By doing this, we're helping to fund the operations of big companies, which in turn creates jobs and supports the economy. On the other hand, if we don't invest our money and instead keep it in cash or buy something like gold, we're not doing much to support the economy. Without our investments, companies wouldn't be able to borrow money from banks or raise money by selling stocks. This would make it much harder for them to operate and grow, and could lead to job losses and economic downturns.

So, as you can see, investing our money is crucial not only for our own financial success, but also for the overall health of our economy. And while our traditional education system may not always teach us everything we need to know about investing, that doesn't mean we can't learn. With the right resources and a willingness to educate ourselves, we can become financially literate and make smart investments that will benefit us and our country. It is important to understand the value of investing our savings in instruments that benefit the economy. Regular savings is a great habit to have, but it is not enough on its own to ensure financial prosperity. The United States of America, for example, has become the world's largest economy due in part to its citizens investing their savings in the country's economy. Similarly, Japan, despite facing the devastating effects of nuclear attacks, has become the third largest economy in the world through the support of its citizens' investments.

The economic growth of a country is directly linked to the financial prosperity of its citizens. This is because when people invest their money in banks and the stock market, it allows companies to access the funds they need to expand their businesses and create employment opportunities. When these companies perform well, they are able to pay back their loans to the banks with interest, and their stock prices increase as a result of their improved performance. It is important to note that this is a cycle of growth and prosperity, where the investments of citizens directly contribute to the success of companies, which in turn benefits the economy and the financial well-being of its citizens. By investing our savings in instruments that benefit the economy, we can not only secure our own financial futures, but also contribute to the overall growth and prosperity of our country.

The problem of financial illiteracy is not only deeply rooted in our education system, but it also limits our potential for financial freedom. Our education system focuses on preparing us to get a good job, earn a decent salary, and buy a house on an EMI plan. While this may provide us with financial security in the short-term, it can also trap us in a cycle of never-ending debt and a lack of financial freedom. The moment we wish to leave our job or pursue something for a greater good, the fear of losing financial security holds us back. The education system rarely teaches us about how to create job opportunities for ourselves and others. There are fundamentally four categories in which people are professionally divided: Employment, Self-

Employment, Business, and Investment. The education system focuses on teaching us about the first two categories, but it completely overlooks the remaining two classes. These last two categories offer an infinite scope for accumulating wealth, while the first two categories are capped by the number of hours a person can work and their skill set.

In other words, when working in the first two categories, one's earning potential is limited to the number of hours they can work and their skills, which is a maximum of 24 hours per day. On the other hand, when one chooses to thrive in the last two categories, they have the potential to earn as much as they want by working as much as they want. People often say "they do what they do because they love it," but this is often an excuse for not investing their time and energy to learn and do the things that will help them achieve what they truly love. In the next chapters of this book, we will delve deeper into understanding the concept of active and passive income, and how it can help us attain financial freedom. It's important to understand that financial freedom is not just about having enough money to live comfortably, but also having the freedom to pursue one's passions and make a positive impact in the world without the fear of losing financial security.

Cognitive Biases: Over Confidence and Sunk Cost Fallacy

One of the most challenging aspects of managing our finances can be making sound financial decisions. Unfortunately, it is all too common for people to make decisions that are not in their best interest, and this can be due in large part to the presence of cognitive biases. Two of the most prevalent and pernicious of these biases are overconfidence and the sunk cost fallacy.

Overconfidence refers to the tendency for people to overestimate their own abilities and the accuracy of their predictions. When it comes to financial decision-making, this can manifest in a number of ways. For example, someone who is overconfident in their investment abilities may make impulsive or risky investments that ultimately lead to financial loss. Similarly, someone who is overconfident in their ability to predict the stock market may make poorly-informed decisions that do not pay off in the long run.

The sunk cost fallacy, on the other hand, refers to the tendency for people to continue to invest in a situation or project even when it is clear that the investment is not paying off. This is because people tend to feel that they have already put so much time, effort, or money into something that they can't bear to let it go. In the context of financial decision-making, this can lead to people continuing to pour money into a failing investment or a losing stock, for example, in the hopes that it will eventually turn around.

Both overconfidence and the sunk cost fallacy can have serious consequences for our financial well-being. It's important to be aware of these biases and to take steps to counteract them. One way to do this is to practice more deliberate, evidence-based decision-making when it comes to our finances. This may include doing more research, seeking out the advice of experts, and carefully considering the potential risks and rewards of a given decision. Additionally, it can be helpful to be mindful of the emotional state when making financial decisions. Emotions like fear, greed, and overconfidence can cloud our judgement and lead us to make poor decisions.

In conclusion, cognitive biases such as overconfidence and the sunk cost fallacy can make it difficult for us to make sound financial decisions. By being aware of these biases and taking steps to counteract them, we can make better, more informed choices when it comes to managing our money.

Chapter 3

Building Mindset for Wealth Creation

There is a common belief that the mindset and attitude towards money and wealth differ between the rich and the poor. The rich are often thought to have a "growth" mentality, while the poor have a "scarcity" mentality.

Growth vs Scarcity Mindset

A growth mentality refers to the belief that there is always an opportunity for growth and success, and that it is possible to create more wealth through hard work and smart decisions. People with a growth mentality tend to focus on long-term goals, invest in themselves and their education, and are willing to take calculated risks to achieve their objectives. They also tend to have a positive attitude towards money and see it as a tool for achieving their goals and improving their lives.

On the other hand, a scarcity mentality refers to the belief that resources, including money, are limited and hard to come by. People with a scarcity mentality tend to focus on short-term goals, are risk-averse, and often believe that they have little control over their financial situation. They tend to be fearful of losing what they have and often have a negative attitude towards money.

It's important to note that having a growth mentality does not guarantee success, and having a scarcity mentality does not guarantee failure. However, research has shown that people with a growth mentality tend to be more successful in their financial lives and are better able to build and maintain wealth over time. It's also important to note that it's not just limited to financial mindset, but also in the way we think, our beliefs and values, and in how we approach life in general. A growth mindset can be developed and nurtured over time, regardless of one's current financial situation. It's never too late to change your mindset and adopt a more positive and proactive approach towards money and wealth.

The scarcity mentality is limiting and negative, often saying things like "this cannot be achieved," "that cannot be done," and "I cannot afford that." These statements reflect a mindset of scarcity and a lack of belief in one's own abilities. On the other hand, the growth mindset is open and positive, and challenges us to think differently and ask questions like "how can this be achieved?", "how can that be done?", and "how can I afford this?" These questions reflect a mindset of abundance and a belief in one's own abilities to find solutions.

The fundamental difference between these two mindsets is that the former one closes the mind, while the later one opens the mind. The scarcity mentality is limiting and it closes one's mind to the possibilities and opportunities, while the growth mentality is empowering and it opens one's mind to the possibilities and opportunities. The growth mentality allows one's brain to exercise and figure out solutions to the problems which can help to achieve financial freedom. This book will help anyone who wants to understand the mindset of the wealthy and learn how to shift from a scarcity mindset to a wealthy one.

The Importance of Financial Planning

The importance of setting financial goals and creating a plan to achieve them cannot be overstated when it comes to managing one's finances and achieving financial success. Having a clear understanding of what one wants to achieve financially, and a plan to get there, can help to provide direction and motivation in making financial decisions.

Setting financial goals is a critical first step in the process of achieving financial success. Goals should be specific, measurable, attainable, relevant, and time-bound (SMART). This means that they should be clear and well defined, with a specific target and a deadline. For example, a specific goal would be to "Save $20,000 for a down payment on a house within 2 years." This goal is specific, measurable, attainable, relevant and time-bound. Creating a plan to achieve these goals is the next step. It's important to break down the goal into smaller, manageable steps and to set up a timeline for achieving each step. This will help to keep the goal on track and make it more manageable. For example, if the goal is to save $20,000 for a down payment on a house within 2 years, the plan would involve creating a budget, setting up automatic savings, and finding ways to increase income.

It's important to regularly review and adjust the plan as needed. Financial goals and circumstances can change over time, so it's important to reassess the plan to ensure that it is still relevant and on track. By regularly reviewing the plan, it will be easier to adjust it as needed to achieve the goals.

In conclusion, setting financial goals and creating a plan to achieve them is a critical step in achieving financial success. It helps to provide direction and motivation in making financial decisions. Goals should be specific, measurable, attainable, relevant, and time-bound, and the plan should be broken down into smaller, manageable steps and regularly reviewed to ensure that it is still on track. It's important to remember that financial success is not a one-time event but a continuous journey that requires discipline, patience and persistence.

The Importance of Budgeting and Money Management

One of the key principles of achieving financial success and building wealth is living below one's means, saving a portion of one's income, and investing for the future. These three practices, when done consistently, can help to create a solid foundation for long-term financial stability and prosperity. Living below one's means means being mindful of how much money is coming in and how much is going out, and making sure that the latter is always less than the former. This requires being mindful of expenses and avoiding frivolous spending or taking on unnecessary debt. By living below one's means, we can ensure that we have enough money to cover our basic needs and have some left over to save and invest for the future.

Saving a portion of one's income is essential for achieving financial success. It is a habit that should be cultivated from a young age. It's important to have an emergency fund to cover unexpected expenses and to have a savings plan for short-term and long-term goals. One of the key benefits of saving is that it allows us to take advantage of opportunities as they arise, rather than being held back by a lack of funds. Investing for the future is also an important aspect of achieving financial success. Investing allows us to grow our money over time and build wealth. It's important to educate oneself on different investment options and to seek advice from professionals to make informed decisions. It's also important to remember that investing is a long-term strategy, and that there will be ups and downs along the way, but staying invested for the long term has a greater chance of success.

When it comes to achieving financial freedom and accumulating wealth, it is not necessarily the amount of money one earns that is important, but rather the amount of money one is able to keep for themselves. It is not uncommon for individuals to earn a high salary or income, but still struggle financially due to poor money management and a lack of financial discipline. One of the key factors to achieving financial freedom is learning how to effectively manage and save your money. This means creating a budget, setting financial goals, and making smart financial decisions. It also means understanding the difference between needs and wants and being able to prioritize spending accordingly. Additionally, it means being mindful of taxes, inflation, and other expenses that can erode your earnings over time. Another important aspect of keeping more of your money is to invest in assets that will generate income for you. This can include investing in stocks, real estate, or starting a business. These types of investments can provide a passive income stream, which can help to cover expenses and increase wealth over time.

Earning a high salary is definitely a good thing, but it is not the only factor in achieving financial freedom. What matters more is how much of that income you are able to keep for yourself by making smart financial decisions, creating a budget, setting financial goals and investing in assets that generate income for you. In conclusion, living below one's means, saving a portion of one's income, and investing for the future are the three key principles that should be followed for achieving financial success. These practices, when done consistently, can help to create a solid foundation for long-term financial stability and prosperity. It's important to keep in mind that financial success is not a one-time event but a continuous journey that requires discipline, patience, and persistence.

Shifting from Saving Mindset to Investing Mindset

One of the key differences between people who struggle financially and those who are financially successful is their mindset when it comes to saving and investing. The traditional way of thinking is to save as much money as possible, in order to have a nest egg for the future or for unexpected expenses. However, this saving mindset can often lead to stagnation and a lack of growth in one's financial situation. On the other hand, an investing mindset focuses on putting money to work for you, rather than simply saving it for a rainy day. This mindset shift can lead to greater financial success, as investments have the potential to grow and generate more income over time.

An investing mindset means actively seeking out opportunities to grow your money, whether it be through stocks, real estate, or other forms of investments. It also means taking calculated risks and being willing to lose some money in order to potentially gain more in the long run. This mindset shift can take time and effort, as it may require learning new skills and gaining knowledge about different types of investments.

In addition, an investing mindset also involves creating a budget and allocating a portion of your income towards investments, rather than only spending it on expenses. This is where the financial discipline equation of (Income - investment = expense) comes in to play. By dedicating a portion of your income towards investments, you are setting yourself up for long-term financial success and potentially achieving financial freedom.

It's important to note that shifting from a saving mindset to an investing mindset doesn't mean neglecting to save at all, but rather finding a balance between saving for short-term needs and investing for long-term growth. By considering both short-term and long-term financial goals and taking a more proactive approach to growing your money, you can set yourself up for financial success.

Developing Financial Discipline (Income – investment = expense)

Financial discipline is the practice of managing one's finances in an organized and responsible way. One of the key components of financial discipline is the ability to understand and adhere to the basic equation of income minus investment equals expenses. Usually, People make the common mistake and follow the equation of income minus expense equals investment. The difference is in the mentality. First think about the investments and then the expenses. This equation is an important tool for understanding the flow of money in one's life and making smart financial decisions.

Income refers to the money that is coming into an individual's life, whether it be from a salary, a business, investments or any other sources. Investment, on the other hand, refers to the money that is being put away or invested in assets that will generate income or appreciate in value. Expenses refer to the money that is being spent on everyday needs and wants. By adhering to this equation, an individual is able to keep track of their income, investment and expenses and make sure that they are in balance. This means ensuring that income is greater than expenses, and that enough money is being invested in assets that will generate income or appreciate in value. By doing this, an individual can ensure that they are living within their means, saving and investing for the future and creating a positive cash flow. Additionally, it is important to note that financial discipline is not just about budgeting and cutting expenses, it's also about having the correct mindset and being mindful about the financial decisions you make. This means recognizing the difference between needs and wants and making smart choices about where to spend your money. It also means developing a long-term financial plan and sticking to it, so that you can achieve your financial goals and ultimately achieve financial freedom.

In summary, Financial discipline is an essential part of achieving financial freedom and is built on the basic equation of income minus investment equals expenses.

Step by Step Process of Getting Rich

The process of becoming wealthy is a multi-step journey that requires a specific mindset, actions and achieving monetary goals.

The first step in the lifecycle of wealthy individuals is to develop the correct mindset for achieving financial freedom. This means understanding the importance of financial discipline, setting clear financial goals, and having a long-term perspective on wealth-building.

The second step is to take the necessary actions to achieve financial freedom. This means making sacrifices and prioritizing the accumulation of assets over the purchase of luxuries. This may require practicing financial discipline, such as budgeting, saving, and investing. Additionally, it's important to generate a positive cash flow by earning more money than you spend, so that you can accumulate assets that generate income.

The third and final step is to achieve one's monetary goals and buy luxury. This is when you have reached a level of financial freedom and can afford to spend money on the luxuries you've been wanting. However, it's important to remember that this step should only be taken after the first two steps have been completed, as it's not sustainable to buy luxuries before achieving financial freedom.

It's common for people to try to skip the first two steps and start buying luxuries in an attempt to look rich. However, this is the wrong approach and leads to a lack of financial stability. It's important to remember that the process of becoming wealthy must be followed in the correct order in order to achieve financial independence and accumulate wealth. By not following the three steps in the correct order, one may end up trapped in a vicious cycle of financial struggles. Wealth brings the privilege of experiencing all the wonderful things life has to offer. It is essential to understand and follow the correct steps in order to become financially independent and enjoy the benefits that come with it.

Chapter 4

Understanding Key Financial Concepts

Understanding key financial concepts is essential for making informed decisions about your money and achieving your financial goals. Some key financial concepts to understand include the following:

Assets and liabilities

Assets and liabilities are two important concepts when it comes to personal finance and accounting. Simply put, assets are things that a person or organization owns that have value, while liabilities are things that a person or organization owes to others.

Assets can include a wide range of items, such as cash, investments, property, and personal possessions. These items can be used to generate income, such as through rental properties or stocks, or they can appreciate in value over time, such as with a piece of real estate or a valuable piece of art.

Liabilities, on the other hand, are obligations that a person or organization owes to others. These can include things like mortgages, car loans, credit card debt, and medical bills. Liabilities are important to consider because they represent money that a person or organization will need to pay back in the future.

When it comes to personal finance, it's important to consider the relationship between assets and liabilities. Essentially, assets can be used to offset liabilities and help to improve a person's overall financial situation. For example, if a person has a large amount of cash saved in a savings account, they may be able to use that money to pay off a credit card balance, which would reduce their overall liabilities.

Another important concept is "Net worth" which is the difference between assets and liabilities, it's a way to measure a person's overall financial health. A positive net worth means that the value of a person's assets is greater than their liabilities, while a negative net worth means that a person's liabilities are greater than their assets.

It's important to regularly review and track both assets and liabilities in order to stay on top of one's financial situation. By keeping a close eye on these numbers, a person can make informed decisions about spending, saving, and investing in order to work towards financial goals.

Active Income vs Passive Income

Active income and passive income are two different ways in which people can earn money. Active income is earned by actively participating in a business or job, typically through a salary or hourly wage. This means that the individual must trade their time and skills for money, and the amount of money they can earn is often limited by the number of hours they are able to work and their level of expertise in their field. For example, if an individual is a teacher, they will only earn money while they are teaching and their income will be capped by their salary and the number of hours they are able to work. Active income is the most common way in which people earn money. It is earned through a job or business that requires the individual to trade their time for money. This means that the more time you put in, the more money you can earn. However, it also means that when you stop working, your income stops as well.

This is where passive income comes into play. Passive income is earned through investments that continue to generate money even when the individual is not actively participating. This can include rental properties, stocks, and other investments that generate a consistent return over time. Passive income can provide a source of income that is not tied to the individual's time and effort, and can potentially generate income even when the individual is not working. Passive income is earned by investing money or time upfront, with the expectation of earning money from the investment in the future. The individual does not need to actively participate in the business or job in order to earn passive income. Some examples of passive income include rental income from a property, dividends from stocks, or interest from a savings account. Passive income can provide a source of income that is not tied to the individual's time and effort, and can potentially generate income even when the individual is not working.

Both active and passive income have their advantages and disadvantages. Active income can provide a consistent and reliable source of income, but it is often tied to the individual's time and effort. Additionally, when the individual stops working, their income stops as well. This means that if an individual wants to increase their income, they must either work more hours or acquire new skills. Passive income, on the other hand, can provide a source of income that is not tied to the individual's time and effort, but it can be more unpredictable and may require a larger initial investment. It is important to note that the distinction between active and passive income is not always clear cut, as there are some forms of income that fall somewhere in between. For example, an individual may earn passive income from a business that they own and operate, but also earn active income by working in the business.

The goal of generating passive income streams is to achieve financial freedom. Financial freedom means having enough income to cover expenses without having to work for a traditional employer. By having multiple streams of passive income, an individual can potentially earn enough money to cover their expenses without having to work for a traditional employer. This can provide a sense of security and freedom, allowing an individual to pursue their passions and goals without being tied down to a specific job or employer. It's important to note that generating passive income requires an initial investment of time and/or money. This can include buying a rental property, investing in stocks, or starting a business. Building a passive income stream takes time and effort, but the long-term benefits can be well worth it.

In conclusion, active income is capped by skills and time, while passive income can provide a source of income that is not tied to the individual's time and effort. The goal of generating passive income streams is to achieve financial freedom, which allows an individual to pursue their passions and goals without being tied down to a specific job or employer. It's important to note that building passive income streams takes time and effort, but the long-term benefits can be well worth it.

Understanding Personal Income Statement:

An income statement is a financial document that outlines a person's financial status. It typically includes four major columns: income, expenses, assets, and liabilities. Income refers to the money a person earns from their job or other sources of income. Expenses are the money a person spends on things such as taxes, loan payments, and other bills. Assets are things that add value to a person's income statement, such as investments or property. Liabilities, on the other hand, are things that subtract from a person's income, such as loans or credit card debt.

Comparing Income Statements of Poor, Middle-Class and Rich

Poor: Poor people typically have a limited income and may struggle to make ends meet. Their income statement may show a low level of revenues, with most of their money going towards basic necessities like food, housing, and transportation. They may also have a high level of expenses, particularly if they have outstanding debts or medical bills. Overall, a poor person's income statement is likely to show a small profit, if any, and may even show a loss.

Middle-class: Middle class people typically have a stable income and may be able to save some money for the future. Their income statement may show a moderate level of revenues, with a significant portion of their money going towards savings and investments. They may also have a moderate level of expenses, particularly if they have a mortgage or car loan. Overall, a middle-class person's income statement is likely to show a small profit, and if they are managing their expenses well, they should be able to save some money for the future.

Rich: Rich people typically have a high income and may have a significant amount of assets and investments. Their income statement may show a high level of revenues, with a significant portion of their money going towards savings, investments, and luxury items. They may also have a low level of expenses, particularly if they own their own home and have paid off any outstanding debts. Overall, a rich person's income statement is likely to show a large profit and they may have substantial savings and investments.

Comparing and contrasting these three types of income statements, one can see that a poor person's income statement is characterized by a high level of expenses and a low level of income, resulting in a negative net income or a loss. In contrast, a rich person's income statement is characterized by a high level of income and relatively low expenses, resulting in a high net income or profit. A middle-class person's income statement falls in between these two extremes, with a balance between income and expenses, resulting in a modest net income. It is important to note that these are generalizations and that individuals may fall into different categories at different points in their lives. Furthermore, income does not always necessarily reflect a person's overall wealth, as a person may have significant wealth in the form of assets such as property or investments, even if their income is relatively low.

Rich people tend to have a strong sense of financial discipline and focus on increasing their assets and decreasing their liabilities. This means that they invest their money in things that will generate more income, such as stocks or real estate, and pay off debt. They also make sure to keep their expenses in check and prioritize saving money over spending. When a person's assets generate enough income to cover their expenses and liabilities, they are considered financially independent. This means that they no longer have to rely on their job or other sources of income to pay their bills. Rich people often strive to achieve this level of financial freedom, as it allows them to live without worrying about money. After achieving financial freedom, rich people may choose to spend money on luxuries, but they are careful to do so without disrupting their positive cash flow. This means that they continue to focus on maintaining their assets and income, and only spend money on things that will not negatively impact their financial stability. In short, rich people have the ability to enjoy their wealth without worrying about money, because they have a good understanding of how to manage their finances.

In summary, the income statement of a poor, middle-class, and rich person can differ significantly. The poor person's income statement may show high expenses and low income resulting in negative net income or loss, a middle-class person's income statement may have a balance of income and expenses resulting in a modest net income, and a rich person's income statement may have a high income and low expenses resulting in a high net income or profit. However, it is important to consider that individuals may fall into different categories at different points in their lives and income does not always necessarily reflect a person's overall wealth.

The Time Value of Money

The time value of money (TVM) is a fundamental concept in finance that refers to the idea that money today is worth more than the same amount of money in the future. This is because money today can be invested and earn interest, whereas money in the future cannot. As a result, the value of money decreases over time due to inflation and opportunity cost.

The concept of time value of money is important in financial decision making, as it helps individuals and businesses to understand the value of their current assets and future cash flows. By considering the time value of money, one can make better financial decisions such as investing in assets that will generate a higher return over time, or choosing to pay off debt sooner rather than later.

The TVM can be understood with the help of the Time Value of Money (TVM) formula, which is used to calculate the present value (PV) or future value (FV) of a stream of cash flows. The PV is the current worth of a future sum of money, and the FV is the future worth of a current sum of money. The TVM formula takes into account the interest rate, or the rate of return, and the number of time periods, such as years or months.

The TVM formula can also be used to calculate net present value (NPV), which is the difference between the present value of the cash inflows and the present value of the cash outflows of an investment. A positive NPV indicates that an investment is expected to generate more cash inflows than cash outflows over a specific period, and thus, it is a worthwhile investment.

In conclusion, the time value of money is a crucial concept that helps individuals and businesses to understand the value of their current assets and future cash flows, and make better financial decisions. By considering the time value of money, one can make more informed decisions about investing, borrowing, or saving money, and ultimately, achieve financial stability and success.

Chapter 5

The Power of Compounding

Introduction

Compounding is the process of earning interest on interest, and it is one of the most powerful financial tools available to us. For example, let's say you have $1000 in a savings account that earns an interest rate of 5% per year. After one year, your account would be worth $1050 (1000+50). If you left the money in the account for another year, you would earn interest not just on the original $1000, but also on the $50 of interest earned in the first year, resulting in an account balance of $1102.50. This process continues to compound over time, resulting in a much larger amount of money than if you had simply left the original $1000 in the account without earning interest. This book explains how compounding can be used to grow wealth over time and how to take advantage of it to achieve financial freedom. It is a powerful and informative guide on how to use the power of compounding to achieve financial success.

The same concept applies to other investments such as stocks and real estate. When investing in stocks, the dividends and capital gains earned on the initial investment also earn interest, resulting in a larger return on the investment over time. Real estate investments can also benefit from compounding through rental income, property appreciation, and tax benefits.

One of the key takeaways from the concept of compounding is the importance of starting early when it comes to saving and investing. The earlier you start investing and saving, the more time your money has to compound and grow. Take an example of two people, one who starts saving at 25 and another who starts at 35. By the time the person who starts at 25 reaches 65, his savings will have grown to be over 4 times larger than the person who starts at 35, even though they both saved the same amount each month. This example illustrates the power of compounding over time and the importance of starting early.

It is extremely crucial to understand the importance of consistency when it comes to saving and investing. Even small amounts of money saved and invested consistently over time can add up to significant sums over the long-term. Take an example of a person who saves $50 per month for 40 years, earning an average annual return of 15%. By the end of the 40 years, that person would have saved more than One million dollars. This example illustrates the power of consistency and the impact it can have on your financial future.

Compounding: The Greatest Discovery in Mathematics of All Time

Compounding is often referred to as the "greatest discovery in mathematics of all time" because of its powerful impact on building wealth over time. One of the most famous examples of the power of compounding is the story of Albert Einstein. He referred to compounding as the "eighth wonder of the world" and said, "he who understands it, earns it; he who doesn't, pays it." This quote highlights the importance of understanding and utilizing the power of compounding in order to build wealth over time.

Rice grain on a chess board

The "Rice grain on chess board story" is a popular analogy used to explain the power of compounding. The story goes like this: A king offers a servant one grain of rice for the first square of a chessboard, two grains for the second square, four grains for the third, and so on, doubling the number of grains for each square until all 64 squares have been filled.

At first, the servant may think the offer is not so great, as the number of grains increases slowly. But as the servant moves through the chessboard, the number of grains increases exponentially. By the time they reach the 64th square, the number of grains has grown to over 18 quintillion! . The wealth of the entire planet would fall short if you want to buy this much amount of rice !

This story illustrates the power of compounding, which is the ability of an asset to generate returns not only on the initial investment, but also on the reinvested returns. The chessboard represents the timeline of an investment, and each square represents a year. The rice grains represent the returns on the investment, which start small but grow larger as the years go by

The key takeaway from this story is that compounding is a powerful force that can turn small investments into large sums over time. The earlier one starts to invest, the more time compounding has to work its magic. It's important to note that, just like the story, the power of compounding takes time to work, and it's not necessarily a get-rich-quick scheme.

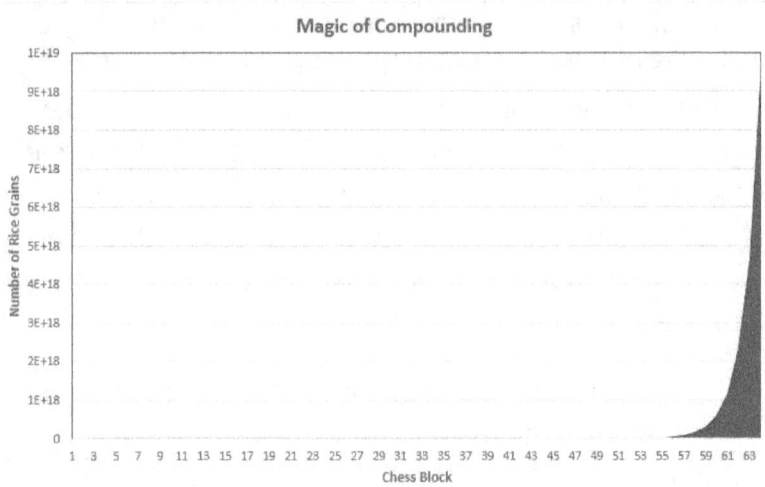

Figure 1: Magic of Compounding

3 Million Dollars Today Vs 1 Dollar Doubling Every Day For 31 Days

The story of "3 million dollars today vs 1 dollar doubling every day for 31 days" is a powerful illustration of the power of compounding. The story goes like this: imagine you have the choice between receiving 3 million dollars today, or receiving 1 dollar on the first day and having it double every day for 31 days. At first glance, 3 million dollars seems like a much better deal. However, if you choose the latter option, by the end of the 31 days, your 1 dollar would have grown to over 10 million dollars. This is the power of compounding at work.

The compounding effect is the process by which an asset or investment grows at a faster rate than the original principal, due to the interest or dividends earned on the principal. In this story, the interest earned on the 1 dollar is reinvested, and earns interest on top of that, leading to exponential growth.

The key takeaway from this story is that the power of compounding can be harnessed to achieve financial goals. This can be done by investing early, investing consistently, and allowing your investments to grow over time. By starting small and allowing your money to grow through compounding, even a small investment can become a significant sum over time.

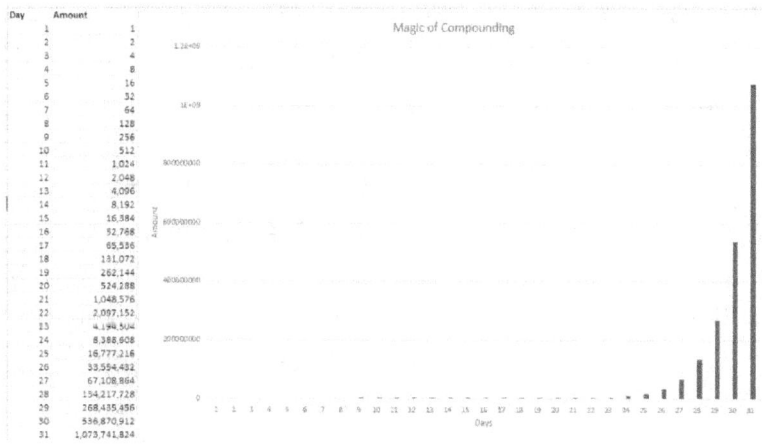

Figure 2 : Magic of Compounding

It is important to remember that compounding is a powerful tool, but it also requires patience, discipline and time. It may not show the immediate results, but with time it will grow and grow, and it's not just a matter of "getting rich quick" but a matter of getting rich smart and consistent. It's also important to note that compounding can work both ways, in a positive and negative way. For example, if you have a debt that's compounding at high interest rates, it can quickly spiral out of control. So, it's also important to be aware of the compounding effect when it comes to managing debt, and to always strive to minimize it.

One of the best ways to take advantage of the power of compounding is through consistent and regular investments in a diversified portfolio of assets, such as stocks, bonds and real estate, that have the potential to generate a return on investment. It's also important to keep an eye on the fees and charges associated with these investments, as they can eat into returns over time. Another important point to consider is the power of compounding is not only applicable to investment but also other aspects of life such as savings, spending and even learning. Consistently saving small amounts of money and investing it into low-cost, diversified investment portfolios over time can lead to significant wealth accumulation. Similarly, consistently learning a new skill or habit can lead to exponential growth over time.

Chapter 6

Warren Buffet's Journey to the Top

Warren Buffett, also known as the "Oracle of Omaha," is a renowned American businessman, investor, and philanthropist who is widely considered to be one of the most successful investors of all time. He is the chairman and largest shareholder of Berkshire Hathaway, a multinational conglomerate holding company. Buffett's story begins in Omaha, Nebraska, where he was born in 1930. From a young age, he showed an interest in business and investing. He would often read annual reports of companies and buy shares in them. By the age of 11, he had already bought his first stock. He continued to invest in the stock market throughout his teenage years and by the time he was 16, he had saved over $6,000 from his paper route and investments. After graduating from the University of Nebraska, Buffett attended the graduate school at Columbia Business School, where he studied under the famous investor Benjamin Graham. It was here that he learned the value investment philosophy which would shape his investing style for the rest of his career.

In the early 1960s, Buffett returned to Omaha and began acquiring a variety of small businesses and investments. He bought a textile company called Berkshire Hathaway and slowly began to turn it into a holding company for his various investments. Over the next few decades, he continued to make savvy investments, particularly in the insurance and energy sectors. He also began to acquire large stakes in well-known companies such as Coca-Cola, American Express, and Wells Fargo. What sets Buffett apart from many other investors is his focus on long-term investments rather than short-term gains.

He has also been a major contributor to charitable organizations and causes, through his philanthropic organization, the Buffett Foundation. He has also pledged to give away the majority of his wealth to charitable causes, primarily through the Giving Pledge, a campaign he started with Bill and Melinda Gates to encourage other billionaires to give away at least half of their wealth to charity. Throughout his life, he has been a strong advocate for philanthropy and has been an inspiration to many people around the world, encouraging them to use their wealth to make a positive impact in their communities and the world. Buffett's philanthropy efforts have been widely praised, and his commitment to giving back has been an important aspect of his legacy. He is an example of how even the wealthiest individuals can make a significant impact on society through charitable giving.

The First Million Dollars

Warren Buffett made his first million dollars through a combination of wise investments, business ventures, and frugal living. One of his early investments was in a textile company called Berkshire Hathaway, which he bought in 1962 for around $8 per share. Over the next several decades, he turned the company into a holding company for his various investments and acquisitions. Through smart investments and shrewd business moves, he was able to grow the value of the company and his own net worth. Buffett also made money through his investment partnerships, which he started in the 1950s. These partnerships allowed him to pool money from investors and make larger investments than he could on his own. He was able to generate high returns for his partners and for himself, which helped him accumulate wealth.

Additionally, Buffett is known for his frugal lifestyle, which allowed him to save and invest a significant portion of his income. He is famously quoted as saying "Rule No. 1: Never lose money. Rule No. 2: Never forget rule No.1"

It's worth noting that it took Buffet a long time to accumulate his first million dollars and his net worth is currently over 100 billion dollars. He didn't achieve it overnight and it took a lot of hard work, patience and smart moves to get there.

The Snowball Effect

Warren Buffett is known for using the power of compounding to create his wealth. Compounding refers to the process of earning interest on top of interest, which can lead to exponential growth over time.

Buffett's investment strategy is centered on the principle of "value investing," which involves identifying undervalued companies with strong fundamentals and holding onto them for the long-term. By investing in these companies and holding onto them for extended periods, he allows the power of compounding to work in his favor. As the companies grow and generate profits, the value of his investment in them also increases, leading to capital appreciation.

Furthermore, Buffet is a long-term investor, he doesn't engage in short-term speculation but instead focuses on holding onto his investments for extended periods of time, allowing the power of compounding to work even more effectively. As the value of his investments increases, the dividend payouts and earnings also increase, leading to even more growth. Buffett's use of compounding can be seen in the tremendous growth of Berkshire Hathaway, the company he bought in 1962 and turned into a holding company for his various investments. Over the years, as he invested in and acquired other companies, the value of Berkshire Hathaway has grown significantly, turning him into a billionaire.

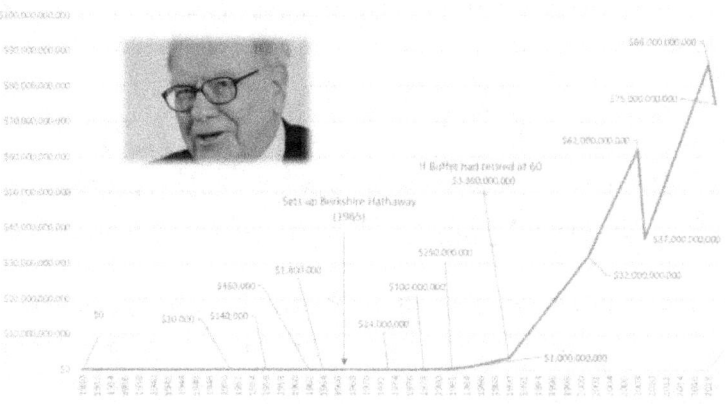

In short, Buffet's use of compounding to create his wealth is a combination of his value investing strategy, long-term focus, and patience. He's a true believer in the power of compounding and it has been a key element in his success as an investor.

Key Takeaways from Warren Buffet's Investment Style

Warren Buffet, often referred to as the "Oracle of Omaha," is one of the most successful investors of all time. His investment style, which focuses on long-term value and a thorough understanding of the companies he invests in, has been the key to his success. Here are some key takeaways from Warren Buffet's investment style:

Focus on Long-Term Disciplined Investing, Avoid Speculation and Emotions

Investing can be a challenging and complex process, but a long-term, patient and disciplined approach can help you navigate the markets and achieve your financial goals. By taking a long-term view, you can focus on the underlying fundamentals of the companies you are investing in, rather than getting caught up in short-term market fluctuations.

A patient approach is also crucial when it comes to investing. Instead of trying to time the market or making impulsive decisions based on the latest news or rumors, it's important to have a well-defined investment strategy and stick to it. This can help you avoid making costly mistakes, such as buying high and selling low, and instead focus on the long-term potential of your investments.

Discipline is also an important aspect of investing. It's important to have a plan in place and stick to it, even when the market is going through a downturn. This can help you avoid succumbing to the emotions of fear and greed that can lead to impulsive decisions. By maintaining a disciplined approach, you can stay focused on your investment goals and avoid making hasty decisions based on short-term market fluctuations.

It's also important to avoid speculative or emotional decisions when investing. Speculation refers to the act of investing in an asset with the expectation of profiting from short-term market fluctuations rather than from the underlying value of the asset. It often involves taking on a high level of risk in the hopes of earning a high return. On the other hand, emotional decisions are often driven by fear or greed, and can lead to impulsive buying or selling, which can be costly in the long run.

In summary, investing can be a challenging and complex process, but a long-term, patient and disciplined approach can help you navigate the markets and achieve your financial goals. By taking a long-term view, being patient and disciplined, and avoiding speculative or emotional decisions, you can increase your chances of success and achieve your financial goals.

Diversify Investments, Don't Put All Eggs in One Basket.

Diversifying investments is an important aspect of financial planning and risk management. It refers to the practice of spreading one's investment capital across a variety of asset classes, sectors, and geographic regions in order to minimize the impact of any one investment performing poorly. This is often referred to as the "not putting all of one's eggs in one basket" principle.

When it comes to investing, it's important to remember that no investment is completely risk-free. Every investment carries some level of risk and the potential for loss. However, by diversifying your investments, you can minimize the impact of any one investment performing poorly. This is because different investments have different risk and return characteristics, and by spreading your money across a variety of different investments, you can reduce the overall risk of your portfolio.

For example, if you only invest in stocks, you are exposed to the risk of the stock market going down. However, if you also invest in bonds, you are exposed to the risk of interest rates going up, but the bond market tends to be less volatile than the stock market, so it can offset some of the risk from the stock market. Additionally, if you diversify your investments across different sectors and geographic regions, you can reduce your exposure to the risk of any one sector or region performing poorly.

Another advantage of diversifying your investments is that it can help you achieve a more consistent return over time. By spreading your money across different investments, you can take advantage of the different returns that each investment provides. This can help you achieve a more consistent return over time and reduce the impact of any one investment performing poorly.

In summary, diversifying investments is an essential aspect of financial planning and risk management. It involves spreading your investment capital across a variety of asset classes, sectors, and geographic regions in order to minimize the impact of any one investment performing poorly. This principle is often referred to as "not putting all of one's eggs in one basket". By diversifying your investments, you can reduce the overall risk of your portfolio and achieve a more consistent return over time.

Risk Management

Financial risk management is the process of identifying, assessing, and mitigating potential financial risks. It is an essential aspect of managing any business or personal finances. The goal of risk management is to minimize the impact of financial risks on the overall financial health and stability of an organization or individual.

There are several types of financial risks, such as credit risk, market risk, operational risk, and strategic risk. Credit risk is the risk of default on a loan or other financial obligation, while market risk is the risk of loss due to changes in market conditions, such as changes in interest rates or currency exchange rates. Operational risk is the risk of loss due to inadequate or failed internal processes, systems, or human error, while strategic risk is the risk of loss due to poor strategic decision making.

To manage financial risks effectively, organizations and individuals must first identify and assess the risks they face. This involves analyzing financial data, conducting risk assessments, and developing risk management strategies. Once potential risks have been identified and assessed, organizations and individuals must implement measures to mitigate or control the risks, such as diversifying investments, purchasing insurance, or implementing risk management systems and procedures.

It's important to note that the process of risk management is ongoing and must be continuously monitored and updated to ensure that the organization or individual is protected against new and emerging risks. Additionally, it's important to keep in mind that no risk management strategy can completely eliminate financial risks, but it can help reduce their impact and minimize the potential for loss.

Moreover, shifting from a saving mindset to an investing mindset is also a key part of effective financial risk management. Saving money is important, but it is not the only way to grow wealth. Investing in assets that generate income, such as stocks, real estate, or businesses, can help create wealth over time. It is a mindset shift that can be difficult for some people, but it is essential for achieving financial freedom and managing financial risks.

PART 2:

Achieving Financial Freedom Through Action

Chapter 7

Learning to do the Math: The First Step Towards Accumulating Wealth

Introduction

In the first part of this book, we delved into the important concept of developing a growth mindset for wealth creation. This mindset, characterized by a willingness to learn, adapt and take calculated risks, is crucial for achieving financial freedom. Now that we have a solid foundation in this area, it's time to equip ourselves with some practical tools that we can use on our journey towards financial independence.

One of the most important tools we can have in our arsenal is a solid understanding of basic financial terms. These terms will be essential when it comes to making calculations and projections related to our finances. One of the best ways to gain this understanding is by using a spreadsheet program like Excel. Excel is a powerful tool that allows us to easily input, manipulate, and analyze data.

In this chapter, we will learn about some of the most commonly used financial terms, and how to use Excel to perform calculations related to them. We will cover concepts such as Present value, Future Value and CAGR. By the end of this chapter, you will have a strong grasp of these concepts and the ability to use Excel to perform calculations related to them. This will be a valuable asset as you continue on your journey towards financial freedom.

It's important to note that while Excel is a great tool for financial calculations, it's not the only one. There are also many other software, mobile apps and online tools that can help you with your financial calculations and keep track of your progress. It's important to find the right tool that works for you, and that you're comfortable using.

In summary, this chapter aims to provide you with a solid understanding of some basic financial terms and the ability to use Excel to perform calculations related to them. This knowledge, combined with the growth mindset we learned about in the first part of the book, will serve as a powerful tool on your journey towards financial freedom.

Using Excel for Financial Calculations

Excel is a powerful tool for financial calculations. It can be used to create financial models, analyze data, and perform various calculations. Some common financial calculations that can be performed in Excel include:

Time Value of Money (TVM) calculations: These calculations can be used to determine the present value, future value, or interest rate of an investment.

Amortization schedules: These schedules can be used to show how much of each payment goes towards paying off the principal and interest on a loan.

Net Present Value (NPV) and Internal Rate of Return (IRR) calculations: These calculations can be used to evaluate the profitability of an investment.

Budgeting and forecasting: Excel can be used to create a budget or forecast future financial performance.

Statistical analysis: Excel can be used to perform various statistical analyses on financial data, such as trend analysis, correlation analysis, and regression analysis.

To perform these calculations, you can use built-in functions such as PMT, FV, PV, IRR, NPV, and many more. It also has built-in charts and graphs which can be used to present the data visually. Excel also allows you to import and manipulate data from external sources, and you can use advanced features such as macros and VBA programming to automate tasks and create custom functions.

Future Value (FV) Of A Single Cash Flow

The future value (FV) of a single cash flow is the amount that a particular cash flow will be worth at a specified point in the future. It takes into account the time value of money, which is the idea that a dollar today is worth more than a dollar in the future due to the potential for earning interest.

Let's say you want to calculate the future value of a $1,000 deposit you plan to make into a savings account that earns an annual interest rate of 5%. We can use the Excel function "FV" to calculate this. The formula for the FV function is:

=FV(rate, nper, pmt, [pv], [type])

Where:

    rate: the interest rate per period (in this case, 5% per year)

    nper: the number of periods (in this case, 5 years)

    pmt: the regular payment (not applicable in this case)

pv: the present value (in this case, $1,000)

type: the timing of the payment (not applicable in this case)

So, to calculate the future value of the $1,000 deposit after 5 years at a 5% annual interest rate, we would enter the following formula into an Excel cell:

=FV(0.05, 5, 0, -1000)

This would return the result of $1,276.28, which is the future value of the deposit after 5 years. This means that after 5 years, the initial deposit of $1,000 will be worth $1,276.28 due to the interest earned on the deposit.

It's important to note that the FV function assumes that interest is compounded annually, but you can use other functions like FV() with different compounding period if you need. Also, you can use the PV function to calculate the present value of future cash flows.

In summary, the future value of a single cash flow is the amount that a particular cash flow will be worth at a specified point in the future, taking into account the time value of money and interest earned. The Excel FV function can be used to easily calculate the future value of a cash flow.

Present Value (PV) Of A Single Cash Flow

The present value (PV) of a single cash flow is the current value of a future cash flow, taking into account the time value of money and an assumed rate of return (discount rate). It represents the amount of money that would be needed today to achieve a certain future cash flow.

Let's say you want to calculate the present value of a $1,000 cash flow that you expect to receive in 5 years. We assume that the discount rate is 5% per year. We can use the Excel function "PV" to calculate this. The formula for the PV function is:

=PV(rate, nper, pmt, [fv], [type])

Where:

> rate: the discount rate per period (in this case, 5% per year)
>
> nper: the number of periods (in this case, 5 years)
>
> pmt: the regular payment (not applicable in this case)
>
> fv: the future value (in this case, $1,000)
>
> type: the timing of the payment (not applicable in this case)

So, to calculate the present value of a $1,000 cash flow that you expect to receive in 5 years, with a discount rate of 5% per year, we would enter the following formula into an Excel cell:

=PV(0.05, 5, 0, 1000)

This would return the result of $778.87, which represents the amount of money that would be needed today to achieve a future cash flow of $1,000 in 5 years, taking into account the time value of money and the discount rate of 5%.

It's important to note that the PV function assumes that the cash flows are received at the end of each period, but you can use other functions like PV() with different compounding period if you need. Also, you can use the FV function to calculate the future value of present cash flows.

In summary, the present value (PV) of a single cash flow is the current value of a future cash flow, taking into account the time value of money and an assumed rate of return (discount rate). The Excel PV function can be used to easily calculate the present value of a cash flow.

Recurring Payment (PMT)

The PMT function in finance is used to calculate the payment (or annuity) of a loan or an investment. PMT stands for "Payment" and it is a built-in function in most spreadsheet software, such as Microsoft Excel and Google Sheets.

The PMT function requires several inputs, including the interest rate, the number of payments, and the present value of the loan or investment. The formula for the PMT function is as follows:

PMT(rate,nper,pv,[fv],[type])

> rate: The interest rate for the loan or investment, expressed as a decimal.
>
> nper: The total number of payments for the loan or investment.
>
> pv: The present value of the loan or investment.
>
> fv: The future value of the loan or investment. This value is optional and is generally set to zero for loans and investments.
>
> type: The number 0 or 1 and indicates when payments are due. 0 for the end of the period, 1 for the beginning of the period.

For example, if a person wants to calculate the monthly payment for a $10,000 loan with a 5% interest rate over a period of 5 years (or 60 months), the PMT function would be:

PMT(0.05/12,60,-10000)

This would give a monthly payment of $177.89. This means that the person would have to pay $177.89 every month for 60 months to repay the loan.

The PMT function is also used to calculate the payment of an annuity, which is a series of equal payments made at regular intervals over a period of time. For example, if an individual wants to calculate the payment for an annuity that will pay $10,000 per year for 20 years, at an interest rate of 4%, the PMT function would be:

PMT(0.04,20,-10000)

This would give a payment of $821.92 per year.

In conclusion, PMT function is a simple, yet powerful tool that allows individuals to calculate the payment for a loan or an annuity. It requires some basic inputs, such as the interest rate, the number of payments, and the present value of the loan or investment. It can be used to calculate both fixed and variable rate loans.

Calculating Rate

The RATE function in Microsoft Excel is a financial function that is used to calculate the interest rate for a loan or investment. The RATE function is a built-in function in Excel, and it is commonly used to calculate the annual interest rate for loans, mortgages, and other types of investments.

The RATE function requires several inputs, including the number of payments, the present value, the future value, and the payment amount. The formula for the RATE function is as follows:

RATE(nper,pmt,pv, [fv], [type], [guess])

> nper: The total number of payments for the loan or investment.
>
> pmt: The payment made each period.
>
> pv: The present value of the loan or investment.
>
> fv: The future value of the loan or investment. This value is optional and is generally set to zero for loans and investments.
>
> type: The number 0 or 1 and indicates when payments are due. 0 for the end of the period, 1 for the beginning of the period.
>
> guess: An estimate for what the rate will be.

For example, if a person wants to calculate the annual interest rate for a $10,000 loan with a monthly payment of $200 for 60 months, the RATE function would be:

RATE(60,-200,-10000)

This would give an annual interest rate of 5.25%. This means that the person would be paying an interest rate of 5.25% on the loan.

The RATE function is also commonly used to calculate the annual interest rate for investments such as bonds or savings accounts. For example, if an individual wants to calculate the annual interest rate for a $5,000 investment that will pay $500 in interest after one year, the RATE function would be:

RATE(1,-500,5000)

This would give an annual interest rate of 10%.

In conclusion, the RATE function in Excel is a powerful tool that allows individuals to calculate the interest rate for a loan or investment. It requires basic inputs, such as the number of payments, the present value, the future value, and the payment amount. It is useful for loan comparison and investment analysis.

Compound Annual Growth Rate (CAGR)

CAGR stands for Compound Annual Growth Rate, which is a measure of the annualized rate of return over a specified period of time. It is used to calculate the average annual growth rate of an investment over a period of time, such as a stock, mutual fund or real estate. The CAGR smooths out the volatility of an investment's returns and provides a single number that represents the average annual return over the period of time.

Let's say you want to calculate the CAGR of a stock investment over the past 5 years. We can use the Excel function "CAGR" to calculate this. The formula for the CAGR function is :

=CAGR(start_value, end_value, number_of_years)

Where:

> start_value: the initial value of the investment (in this case, $10,000)
>
> end_value: the final value of the investment (in this case, $15,000)
>
> number_of_years: the number of years over which the investment has grown (in this case, 5)

So, to calculate the CAGR of a stock investment that started at $10,000 and ended at $15,000 over a period of 5 years, we would enter the following formula into an Excel cell:

=CAGR(10000, 15000, 5)

This would return the result of 12.18%, which represents the average annual growth rate of the investment over the past 5 years.

It's important to note that CAGR is an effective way of measuring the growth of an investment over time, but it has some limitations. It assumes that the investment compounds annually and that the returns are reinvested. Also, CAGR doesn't take into account the volatility of the investment and could be misleading in case of investments with higher volatility.

In summary, CAGR is a measure of the annualized rate of return over a specified period of time, which is used to calculate the average annual growth rate of an investment over a period of time. The Excel CAGR function can be used to easily calculate the CAGR of an investment.

Internal Rate of Return (IRR)

The IRR function in Microsoft Excel is a financial function that is used to calculate the internal rate of return (IRR) for a series of cash flows that occur at regular intervals. The IRR function is a built-in function in Excel and it can be used to calculate the internal rate of return for investments such as bonds, stocks, and real estate.

The IRR function requires one input: a range of cash flows, which can be positive (inflow) or negative (outflow). The formula for the IRR function is as follows:

IRR(values, [guess])

> values: A range of cash flows, which can be positive (inflow) or negative (outflow).
>
> guess: An estimate of what the IRR will be (a percentage), which is optional.

For example, if an individual wants to calculate the internal rate of return for an investment that had cash flows of -$1000 at the beginning of the year, $300 at the end of the first year, $500 at the end of the second year and $700 at the end of the third year. The IRR function would be:

IRR({-1000,300,500,700})

This would give an internal rate of return of 20.3%. This means that the investment had an annual return of 20.3%.

The IRR function is useful when the cash flows are regular, unlike the XIRR function which can be used for irregular cash flows. It's commonly used for investment analysis, such as bonds, stocks, and real estate.

In conclusion, the IRR function in Excel is a useful tool that allows individuals to calculate the internal rate of return for a series of cash flows that occur at regular intervals. It requires one input: a range of cash flows. It's commonly used for investment analysis, such as bonds, stocks, and real estate. It's important to note that IRR has some limitations, such as assuming regular cash flows, not considering the time value of money, also it can be affected by the magnitude and timing of cash flows.

XIRR

The XIRR function in Microsoft Excel is a financial function that is used to calculate the internal rate of return (IRR) for a series of cash flows that occur at irregular intervals. The XIRR function is a built-in function in Excel and it can be used to calculate the internal rate of return for investments such as stocks, mutual funds, and real estate.

The XIRR function requires two inputs: a range of cash flows and a range of dates corresponding to those cash flows. The formula for the XIRR function is as follows:

XIRR(values, dates, [guess])

> values: A range of cash flows, which can be positive (inflow) or negative (outflow).

dates: A range of dates corresponding to the cash flows. The dates must be entered in the Excel serial number format (e.g. "1/1/2022" would be entered as "43221").

guess: A guess for the internal rate of return, which is optional.

For example, if an individual wants to calculate the internal rate of return for an investment in a stock that had cash flows of $1000 on January 1st 2022, $2000 on June 1st 2022, and $3000 on December 1st 2022. The XIRR function would be:

XIRR({-1000,2000,3000},{43221,43287,43352})

This would give an internal rate of return of 20.3%. This means that the investment had an annual return of 20.3%.

The XIRR function is useful when the cash flows are irregular, unlike the IRR function which assumes regular cash flows. It also allows for multiple inflow and outflow of cash.

In conclusion, the XIRR function in Excel is a powerful tool that allows individuals to calculate the internal rate of return for a series of cash flows that occur at irregular intervals. It requires two inputs: a range of cash flows and a range of dates corresponding to those cash flows. It's commonly used for investment analysis, such as stocks, mutual funds, and real estate.

Future Value of Annuity

The future value of an annuity refers to the total amount of money that will accumulate in an account over a certain period of time, given a fixed rate of return and a set amount of regular contributions. An annuity is a financial product that pays out a fixed amount of money at regular intervals, typically monthly or annually. The future value of an annuity is an important concept for anyone looking to save or invest money over a long period of time, such as for retirement.

The formula for calculating the future value of an annuity is: FV = PMT x (((1 + r)^n - 1) / r)

Where: FV = Future value of the annuity PMT = The fixed payment made at regular intervals r = The interest rate, expressed as a decimal n = The number of payments or intervals

For example, if you invest $100 per month at a 5% annual interest rate for 20 years, the future value of your annuity would be $48,939. This means that your investment will grow to $48,939 over the course of 20 years, assuming you make a consistent investment of $100 per month and earn a 5% annual interest rate.

It's important to note that the future value of an annuity is affected by several factors, including the regular contribution amount, the interest rate, and the length of time the investment is held. In general, the higher the interest rate and the longer the investment is held, the greater the future value of the annuity will be.

Additionally, there is a concept called Annuity Due which is slightly different from ordinary annuity. The payment of Annuity Due is made at the beginning of the period instead of at the end.

It's crucial to understand the future value of an annuity concept when planning for long-term financial goals like retirement. It helps an individual to know how much they should be saving and investing regularly to achieve their future financial goals.

Present Value of Annuity

The present value of an annuity refers to the current value of a series of future payments or cash flows, given a certain interest rate. It is the opposite of future value, which looks at how much money will accumulate over time. The present value of an annuity is used to determine the value of an investment today, based on the future cash flows it will provide.

The formula for calculating the present value of an annuity is: PV = PMT x (1 - (1 + r)^-n) / r

Where: PV = Present value of the annuity PMT = The fixed payment made at regular intervals r = The interest rate, expressed as a decimal n = The number of payments or intervals

For example, if you are offered an investment that pays $1,000 per year for 10 years at a 5% annual interest rate, the present value of the annuity would be $8,167. This means that the investment is worth $8,167 today, based on the future cash flows of $1,000 per year for 10 years and a 5% annual interest rate.

It's important to note that the present value of an annuity is affected by several factors, including the regular payment amount, the interest rate, and the length of time until the payments are received. In general, the lower the interest rate and the longer the time until the payments are received, the higher the present value of the annuity will be.

Similar to Future Value, Present Value of Annuity Due is slightly different from an ordinary annuity. The present value of an annuity due is calculated by discounting the future cash flows back to the present time, but assuming that the first cash flow is received at the beginning of the first period, rather than the end.

The present value of an annuity concept is important for investors and financial professionals to evaluate the current value of an investment. It is also used by businesses to determine the value of future cash flows from a project, such as a new product launch or a real estate investment.

Constant Perpetuity

A constant perpetuity is a financial concept that refers to a stream of constant cash flows that continue indefinitely into the future. It is a type of annuity where the payments or cash flows are fixed and occur at regular intervals, such as annually or monthly, and continue indefinitely without any end date.

The formula for calculating the present value of a constant perpetuity is: $PV = C / r$

Where: PV = Present value of the perpetuity C = The fixed cash flow or payment r = The discount rate or interest rate, expressed as a decimal

For example, if a company is expected to pay a constant dividend of $1 per share every year indefinitely, and the discount rate is 5%, the present value of the perpetuity would be $20 per share. This means that the stream of dividends is currently worth $20 per share, based on the assumption that the dividends will continue indefinitely at $1 per share and the discount rate of 5%.

It's important to note that the present value of a constant perpetuity is sensitive to the discount rate. As the discount rate increases, the present value decreases, and as the discount rate decreases, the present value increases.

It's also important to note that the concept of constant perpetuity is highly theoretical and unrealistic. In practice, cash flows and dividends are subject to change and may not continue indefinitely. Additionally, the discount rate used in the present value calculation is usually estimated using the prevailing market interest rate, which can also change over time.

Constant perpetuities are used in financial analysis and valuation, usually as a theoretical construct, to help understand and compare the relative value of different investments or financial products. It's important to understand the assumptions and limitations of this concept when using it in financial analysis.

Growing perpetuity

A growing perpetuity is a financial concept that refers to a stream of cash flows that continue indefinitely into the future, with the cash flows growing at a constant rate. It is a type of annuity where the payments or cash flows are not fixed but grow at a constant rate. The payments occur at regular intervals, such as annually or monthly, and continue indefinitely without any end date.

The formula for calculating the present value of a growing perpetuity is: $PV = C / (r - g)$

Where: PV = Present value of the perpetuity C = The initial cash flow or payment r = The discount rate or interest rate, expressed as a decimal g = The growth rate of the cash flows, also expressed as a decimal

For example, if a company is expected to pay a dividend of $1 per share next year, with the dividends growing at a rate of 3% annually, and the discount rate is 5%, the present value of the perpetuity would be $20 per share. This means that the stream of dividends, which is currently worth $20 per share, based on the assumption that the dividends will continue to grow at a rate of 3% annually and the discount rate of 5%.

It's important to note that the present value of a growing perpetuity is sensitive to the discount rate and the growth rate. As the discount rate increases, the present value decreases, and as the discount rate decreases, the present value increases. Similarly, as the growth rate increases, the present value of the perpetuity increases, and as the growth rate decreases, the present value decreases.

Like the constant perpetuity, Growing perpetuity concept is also highly theoretical and unrealistic. In practice, cash flows and dividends are subject to change and may not continue indefinitely. Additionally, the discount rate used in the present value calculation is usually estimated using the prevailing market interest rate, which can also change over time.

Growing perpetuities are used in financial analysis and valuation, usually as a theoretical construct, to help understand and compare the relative value of different investments or financial products. It's important to understand the assumptions and limitations of this concept when using it in financial analysis.

Growing annuity

A growing annuity is a financial concept that refers to a stream of cash flows that occur at regular intervals, such as annually or monthly, but unlike a perpetuity, these cash flows have a finite end date. The cash flows grow at a constant rate over the life of the annuity.

The formula for calculating the present value of a growing annuity is: $PV = C*(1-(1+g/n)^{(-nt)})/(r-g)$

Where: PV = Present value of the growing annuity C = The initial cash flow or payment r = The discount rate or interest rate, expressed as a decimal g = The growth rate of the cash flows, also expressed as a decimal n = The number of compounding periods per year t = The number of years the cash flows will occur

For example, if a company is expected to pay a dividend of $1 per share next year, with the dividends growing at a rate of 3% annually, for the next 10 years, and the discount rate is 5% and number of compounding periods per year is 1 then the present value of the growing annuity would be $17.28 per share.

It's important to note that the present value of a growing annuity is sensitive to the discount rate and the growth rate. As the discount rate increases, the present value decreases, and as the discount rate decreases, the present value increases. Similarly, as the growth rate increases, the present value of the growing annuity increases, and as the growth rate decreases, the present value decreases.

Growing Annuity concept is also theoretical but less unrealistic as compared to perpetuities as it has a finite end date. In practice, cash flows and dividends are subject to change and may not continue indefinitely. Additionally, the discount rate used in the present value calculation is usually estimated using the prevailing market interest rate, which can also change over time.

Growing annuities are used in financial analysis and valuation, usually as a theoretical construct, to help understand and compare the relative value of different investments or financial products. It's important to understand the assumptions and limitations of this concept when using it in financial analysis.

Retirement planning

We will now apply the financial concepts we have learnt so far to create a retirement plan for the following scenario:

"I am a 20 year old, my monthly expenses are 5000 $. I will retire at the age of 60. Life expectancy is 90 years. What is the amount of money that I need to deposit/invest every month in bank (starting one month from now, till the age of 60) to accumulate the required retirement corpus that would be sufficient to meet my needs for the age of 60 to 90 Assumption: the retirement corpus would be kept in the bank at 7% CAGR and the inflation rate is 5%"

To create a retirement plan using excel, we will first calculate the total expenses for the time period of age 60 to 90. We will also take into account the inflation rate of 5%. We can do this by multiplying the monthly expenses of $5000 by 12 (months) and then multiplying that result by 30 (years) and then multiplying that result with 1.05^30 (1+inflation rate)^number of years. This gives us a total expenses of $41,928,867.

Next, we will use the formula for future value of an annuity to calculate the amount of money that needs to be deposited/invested every month in order to reach the desired retirement corpus. The formula is:

FV = PMT * (((1 + r)^n - 1) / (r-g))

Where:

> PMT = the deposit/investment amount per month
>
> r = the interest rate (in this case, 0.07 or 7%)
>
> n = the number of months till retirement (in this case, (60-20)*12 = 480)
>
> g = the growth rate or inflation rate (in this case, 0.05 or 5%)

Using this formula, we can calculate the PMT. After putting the values in the formula:

PMT = FV / (((1 + 0.07)^480 - (1+0.05)^480) / (0.07-0.05))

PMT = 41,928,867 / (((1 + 0.07)^480 - (1+0.05)^480) / (0.07-0.05))

PMT = $5,716.87

Therefore, in order to accumulate the required retirement corpus of $41,928,867 by the age of 60, you need to deposit/invest $5,716.87 every month starting one month from now taking into account the inflation rate of 5%.

We can then use excel functions like PMT, FV, NPER and RATE to calculate the same.

To summarize, a 20-year-old person needs to deposit/invest $5,716.87 per month starting one month from now till the age of 60 to reach the retirement corpus of $41,928,867 which would be sufficient to meet the expenses from age 60 to 90 assuming 7% CAGR, 5% inflation rate and life expectancy of 90 years.

Chapter 8

The Wealth Creation Hut

Introduction

The Wealth Creation Hut is a powerful concept that helps individuals understand the art of creating wealth in the long term. At the core of this concept is the idea that insurance is the foundational and most essential piece of wealth creation. Without proper insurance, individuals and their families are at risk of financial ruin in the event of an unexpected medical or life event.

The second piece of the Wealth Creation Hut is the left pillar, which represents active income. This pillar emphasizes the importance of increasing one's knowledge and skills in order to maximize active income. This can be achieved through education and training, as well as by seeking out new opportunities for growth and advancement in one's career.

The third piece of the Wealth Creation Hut is the right pillar, which represents portfolio building. This pillar emphasizes the importance of regular investments of savings from active income in order to build a diverse portfolio of assets. This can include stocks, bonds, real estate, and other investment vehicles. By building a portfolio, individuals can generate passive income from their investments, which can provide a steady stream of income even after they have retired.

The fourth piece of the Wealth Creation Hut is the roof, which represents passive income. This type of income is derived from portfolio income and other sources such as rental income, royalties, and dividends. Passive income is a powerful tool for creating long-term wealth, as it provides a steady stream of income that can be used to support one's lifestyle or to invest in further wealth-building opportunities.

The fifth and final piece of the Wealth Creation Hut is the cap, which represents a second income. This type of income is not passive, but rather a part-time income such as freelancing, consulting, or a side hustle. This income is like a cherry on top of the cake, as it provides an additional source of income that can be used to supplement one's active income and further accelerate the wealth-building process.

Overall, the Wealth Creation Hut is a powerful concept that can help individuals create wealth in the long term by focusing on the key elements of insurance, active income, portfolio building, passive income and a second income. By understanding and implementing the principles of the Wealth Creation Hut, individuals can take control of their financial future and achieve their long-term wealth-building goals.

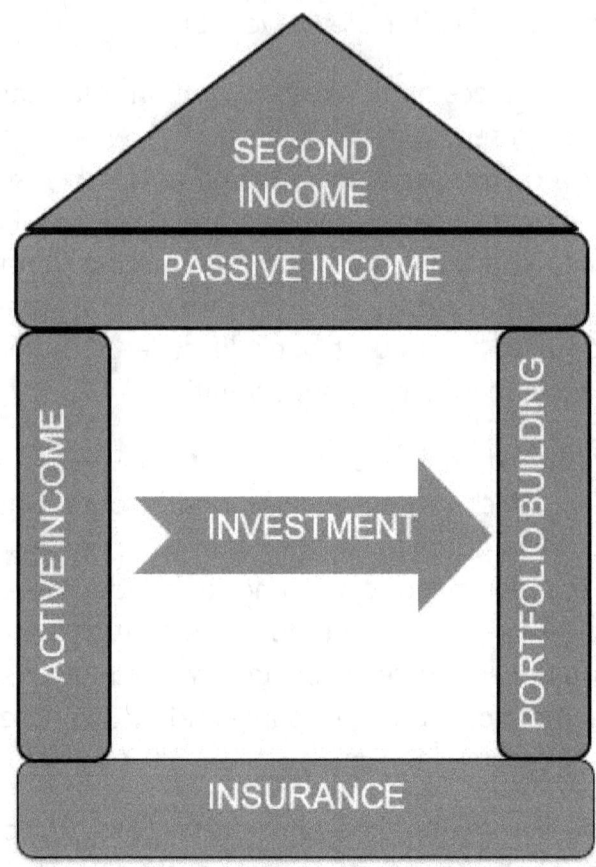

Insurance

Insurance is a crucial component of personal finance that provides financial protection against unexpected events. It is an essential tool for managing risk and ensuring financial security for individuals and their families. Without insurance, individuals are at risk of financial ruin in the event of an unexpected medical or life event.

There are different types of insurance, each of which serves a specific purpose. For example, health insurance helps cover the cost of medical expenses, while life insurance provides financial protection for one's loved ones in the event of a premature death. Other types of insurance include auto insurance, homeowner's insurance, and disability insurance.

Health insurance is one of the most important types of insurance, as it helps protect individuals and their families against the high cost of medical care. Without health insurance, an unexpected illness or injury could result in financial ruin. Health insurance can help cover the cost of doctor's visits, hospital stays, and prescription drugs, and can also provide access to preventative care, such as regular check-ups and screenings.

Life insurance is another important type of insurance that can provide financial protection for loved ones in the event of the policyholder's premature death. It can help cover the cost of funeral expenses, pay off outstanding debts, and provide a source of income for one's beneficiaries. Without life insurance, a family may struggle to make ends meet in the event of a premature death of the primary breadwinner.

Auto insurance is mandatory in most states, as it helps protect individuals from financial losses in the event of an accident. It can cover the cost of repairs to one's vehicle as well as medical expenses for injuries sustained in an accident. Without auto insurance, an accident could result in significant financial losses.

Homeowners insurance is a must for people who own a house, as it helps protect against financial losses due to damage or destruction of one's home and personal property. It can also provide liability coverage in the event that someone is injured on your property. Without homeowners insurance, a natural disaster or other catastrophic event could result in significant financial losses.

Disability insurance is a type of insurance that provides income replacement for individuals who are unable to work due to a disability. It is an important form of insurance for people who rely on their income to support themselves and their families. Without disability insurance, a sudden injury or illness could result in a significant loss of income.

In conclusion, insurance is an essential aspect of personal finance that helps protect individuals and their families against unexpected events. It can help cover the cost of medical expenses, provide financial protection for loved ones, and protect against financial losses due to accidents or other events. By having the right types of insurance, individuals can manage risk, secure financial stability and focus on their long-term goals.

Why Not to Mix Insurance with Investment

When it comes to personal finance, it is important to understand the difference between insurance and investment. While both can play a role in achieving financial security, they serve distinct purposes and should not be mixed together.

Insurance is a risk management tool that helps protect individuals and their families against unexpected events, such as medical expenses or premature death. The purpose of insurance is to provide financial protection in the event of an unforeseen loss.

Investment, on the other hand, is a way to grow one's wealth over time. The purpose of investment is to earn a return on one's money by investing in assets such as stocks, bonds, and real estate.

Mixing insurance and investment can lead to confusion and can potentially harm one's financial well-being. For example, some insurance products, such as whole life insurance, are sold as a combination of insurance and investment. However, these types of products often have high fees, and the returns on the investment portion may be lower than what could be achieved through other types of investments. Additionally, these types of products often require a commitment to pay premiums for a long period of time, which may not be suitable for one's financial situation.

Another example is investing in insurance-linked securities, which are securities that are tied to the performance of an insurance company or a specific insurance product. It's not suitable for most of the investors and not recommended for the general public as it requires a deep understanding of the insurance market and the underlying risks.

It is important to understand that insurance and investment are two distinct concepts, and each serves a specific purpose. Insurance is a risk management tool that provides financial protection, while investment is a way to grow one's wealth over time. By keeping insurance and investment separate, individuals can better manage their financial risks and achieve their long-term financial goals.

In conclusion, when it comes to personal finance, it is important to understand the difference between insurance and investment and not to mix them. Each serves a specific purpose, and mixing them can lead to confusion and potentially harm one's financial well-being. By keeping insurance and investment separate, individuals can better manage their financial risks and achieve their long-term financial goals.

Active Income

Active income is the money that individuals earn through their work, such as wages, salaries, and commissions. It is important to maximize active income because it can provide the foundation for achieving financial security and reaching long-term financial goals. People can be broadly classified into four classes based on their earning styles i.e., Employed, Self-Employed, Business owner, Investor.

Employed

If you are an employee, there are several ways to maximize your active income. One of the most effective ways is to increase your knowledge and skills. This can be done through education, training, and professional development. For example, pursuing additional education or certification can open up new job opportunities with higher pay. Furthermore, staying current with industry trends and advancements can increase your value in the job market.

Another way to maximize your active income is to negotiate for higher pay. This can be done by researching the going rates for similar positions in the same industry and highlighting your qualifications and value to your employer during salary negotiations. It's also important to be ready to demonstrate how your work has been beneficial to the company and what are the future plans to keep adding value.

Networking is another key strategy to maximize active income. Building a strong network of professional contacts can open up new job opportunities and lead to higher pay. Networking can also provide valuable information and advice on how to advance in one's career.

You can also seek out opportunities for advancement within your current company. This can include taking on additional responsibilities, leading projects, or working on high-profile initiatives. By demonstrating your value to the company, you may be able to negotiate a higher salary or position.

Additionally, It's important to keep in mind that maximizing active income also requires balancing work and personal life. Working too much can lead to burnout, which can negatively impact one's health and well-being, and thus negatively impact the income in the long run.

In conclusion, as an employee, you can maximize your active income by increasing your knowledge and skills, negotiating for higher pay, networking, seeking out opportunities for advancement, and balancing work and personal life. By taking these steps, you can increase your active income, which can provide the foundation for reaching long-term financial goals.

Self-Employed

If you are self-employed, there are several ways to maximize your active income. One of the most important ways is to focus on building a strong and loyal customer base. This can be done by providing excellent customer service, developing a unique value proposition, and building a strong online presence through social media and other digital marketing strategies. Additionally, creating a strong network of industry contacts can open up new business opportunities.

Another way to maximize your active income is to diversify your revenue streams. This can include offering new products or services, expanding into new markets, or developing new business models.

Diversifying your revenue streams can help to reduce risk and increase the overall stability of your business.

It's also important to be aware of the costs of running your business and look for ways to reduce them. This can include cutting unnecessary expenses, negotiating better deals with suppliers, and investing in technology and automation to streamline operations.

In addition, it's important to continuously improve your skills and knowledge in your field. This can be done by attending industry conferences, workshops, and networking events, as well as staying current with industry trends and best practices.

Another strategy is to leverage your time and work smarter, not harder. This can include outsourcing non-core tasks, automating repetitive processes, and creating systems and procedures to increase efficiency.

Finally, seeking out business funding, such as small business loans or crowdfunding, can also help to maximize your active income. This can provide the necessary capital to invest in growth opportunities or weather economic downturns.

In conclusion, as a self-employed individual, you can maximize your active income by building a strong and loyal customer base, diversifying your revenue streams, reducing costs, continuously improving your skills and knowledge, leveraging your time and seeking out business funding. By taking these steps, you can increase your active income, which can provide the foundation for reaching long-term financial goals.

Business Owner

As a business owner, maximizing your active income is essential for the growth and success of your company. Active income refers to the income earned through actively participating in your business operations, such as through sales or services provided. In this chapter, we will discuss several strategies for maximizing your active income as a business owner.

Diversify your revenue streams: One of the most effective ways to maximize your active income is to diversify your revenue streams. Instead of relying on one main source of income, diversifying allows you to tap into multiple streams, which can help mitigate the risk of losing a significant portion of your revenue if one stream dries up. For example, if you own a retail store, consider offering online sales or renting out space to other businesses.

Increase your prices: Another way to increase your active income is to raise your prices. As long as your prices are still competitive and your products or services are of high quality, raising your prices can increase your revenue without having to increase your sales volume. However, it's important to note that you should not increase your prices too drastically or too frequently as it could lead to losing your customers.

Expand your customer base: Expanding your customer base is another effective way to maximize your active income. By reaching new customers, you can increase your sales and revenue without having to rely on existing customers alone. This can be done through targeted marketing campaigns, networking, or partnerships with other businesses.

Optimize your pricing strategy: To maximize your active income, it's important to have a pricing strategy that is optimized for your products or services. This means considering factors such as production costs, market demand, and competition when setting your prices. A well-optimized pricing strategy can help ensure that you are charging the right amount for your products or services, which can lead to increased revenue.

Create recurring revenue: Another strategy for maximizing your active income is to create recurring revenue streams. This can be done by offering subscription-based services or products, such as a monthly membership or a recurring delivery service. Recurring revenue streams provide a steady stream of income and can help mitigate the risk of losing revenue if sales slow down.

In conclusion, maximizing your active income as a business owner is crucial for the growth and success of your company. By diversifying your revenue streams, increasing your prices, expanding your customer base, optimizing your pricing strategy and creating recurring revenue, you can increase your revenue and achieve long-term success. It's important to keep in mind that these strategies must be implemented in a smart and strategic manner, with careful consideration of the current market trends and customer behavior.

Investor

As an investor, maximizing your active income is crucial for achieving your financial goals. Active income, in the context of investing, refers to the income earned through actively managing your investments, such as through dividends, interest, or capital gains. In this chapter, we will discuss several strategies for maximizing your active income as an investor.

Invest in dividend-paying stocks: One of the most effective ways to earn active income as an investor is to invest in dividend-paying stocks. Dividend-paying stocks are stocks of companies that pay a portion of their profits to shareholders in the form of dividends. These dividends provide a steady stream of income, which can be reinvested or used to supplement other sources of income.

Invest in bonds: Another strategy for maximizing your active income as an investor is to invest in bonds. Bonds are debt securities that pay a fixed rate of interest to investors. These interest payments provide a steady stream of income and can be a reliable source of active income for investors.

Invest in real estate: Real estate is another asset class that can provide a steady stream of active income. This can be done through investing in rental properties, which can generate rental income, or through investing in real estate investment trusts (REITs), which are publicly traded companies that own and operate real estate properties.

Invest in peer-to-peer lending: Peer-to-peer (P2P) lending is a relatively new investment opportunity that allows investors to earn active income by lending money to borrowers. This is done through online platforms, which connect borrowers and lenders. As a lender, you can earn a higher return on your investment than what you would earn through traditional savings accounts or bonds.

Invest in business opportunities: Another way to maximize your active income as an investor is to invest in business opportunities. This can be done by investing in a small business or becoming a silent partner in an existing business. This can provide you with a share of the business' profits and can be a great way to earn active income.

In conclusion, maximizing your active income as an investor is crucial for achieving your financial goals. By investing in dividend-paying stocks, bonds, real estate, peer-to-peer lending, and business opportunities, you can generate a steady stream of income and achieve long-term financial success. It's important to keep in mind that these strategies should be implemented as part of a diversified investment portfolio and with careful consideration of your risk tolerance and investment goals.

Portfolio Building

Building wealth is an important goal for many individuals, and there are a variety of ways to accumulate assets and create a solid wealth portfolio. One of the most important things to keep in mind when building wealth is the importance of diversification. This means spreading your investments across different types of assets, such as stocks, bonds, real estate, and cash. By diversifying your portfolio, you can reduce your overall risk and increase your chances of achieving long-term financial success.

One way to start accumulating assets is by investing in stocks. Stocks represent ownership in a company, and as the company grows and becomes more profitable, the value of the stock typically increases. Investing in a diversified mix of stocks can provide a good return on investment over time. However, it's important to remember that stock prices can be volatile and there is a risk of losing money.

Another way to accumulate assets is through real estate investing. This can include purchasing rental properties, flipping houses, or investing in real estate investment trusts (REITs). Real estate can provide a steady stream of passive income and has the potential for significant appreciation over time. However, it's important to keep in mind that real estate investing also comes with risks, such as market fluctuations, property maintenance costs, and the potential for vacancies.

Bonds are another option for diversifying your portfolio. Bonds are essentially loans that are made to governments, municipalities, and corporations. When you purchase a bond, you are lending money to the issuer in exchange for regular interest payments and the return of the principal at the end of the bond's term. Bonds are generally considered less risky than stocks, but they also tend to offer lower returns.

Another important aspect of building wealth is to save and invest consistently over time. This can be achieved by setting up automatic contributions to a savings or investment account, and by avoiding unnecessary purchases. It's also important to have an emergency fund to cover unexpected expenses.

Another aspect is to minimize your debt as much as possible. High-interest debt, such as credit card debt, can be a significant burden on your finances and can make it difficult to save and invest for the future. It's important to pay off high-interest debt as quickly as possible, and to avoid taking on new debt whenever possible.

In summary, there are many ways to accumulate assets and build a solid wealth portfolio. It's important to diversify your investments, invest consistently over time, minimize your debt, and to have an emergency fund. Keep in mind that building wealth takes time and effort, but by following these strategies and being patient, you can achieve your financial goals.

Passive Income

Generating passive income is a great way to create a sustainable source of income that can provide financial freedom and security. There are many different ways to generate passive income, including rental income, portfolio income, online courses, drop shipping, eBooks, social media, and royalties.

Rental Income

Rental income is generated by renting out property or assets to others. This can include anything from a spare room in your house to a storage unit or even a piece of equipment. The key to generating rental income is to find a property or asset that is in high demand and that can be rented out at a competitive rate. This can include anything from a single-family home, apartment, or commercial property, to boats, RVs, or storage units. Once you have found a property or asset that is in demand, you can either manage the property yourself or hire a property management company to handle the day-to-day operations.

Portfolio Income

Portfolio Income is generated by investing in stocks, bonds, mutual funds, and other types of securities. The key to generating portfolio income is to invest in a diverse range of securities that have the potential to generate a return over time. This can include anything from blue-chip stocks to emerging market bonds. The key to generating portfolio income is to diversify your investments and to invest for the long-term.

Online Courses

Creating and selling online courses is another way to generate passive income. Online courses can be created on any topic, from cooking to coding, and can be sold through platforms like Udemy, Coursera, and Skillshare. The key to generating income through online courses is to create a high-quality course that is in demand and that can be sold at a competitive price.

Drop shipping

Drop shipping is a business model in which you sell products to customers without ever holding inventory. Instead, you partner with a supplier who holds the inventory and ships the products directly to your customers. The key to generating income through drop shipping is to find a profitable niche, source products from a reliable supplier, and market your products effectively.

eBooks

Writing and selling eBooks is another way to generate passive income. eBooks can be created on any topic and can be sold through platforms like Amazon Kindle Direct Publishing, Google Play Books, and Apple Books. The key to generating income through eBooks is to write a high-quality book that is in demand and that can be sold at a competitive price.

Social Media

Social media platforms like Instagram, TikTok, and YouTube can be used to generate passive income through sponsorships, affiliate marketing, and advertising. The key to generating income through social media is to build a large following and to create high-quality content that is engaging and in demand.

Royalties

Royalties are a form of income that is generated through the sale or use of a product or service. This can include anything from the sale of a book or song, to the use of a piece of artwork or software. The key to generating royalties is to create a high-quality product or service that is in demand and that can be licensed or sold at a competitive price.

20 More Ways to Generate Passive Income

1. Peer-to-peer lending: Investing in peer-to-peer lending platforms like Lending Club and Prosper allows you to lend money to borrowers and earn interest on your investment.

2. Investing in a podcast network: Investing in a podcast network can provide passive income through advertising and sponsorship.

3. Real estate crowdfunding: Investing in real estate crowdfunding platforms like Fundrise and RealtyMogul allows you to invest in real estate projects and earn rental income and capital appreciation.

4. Virtual assistant: Setting up a virtual assistant business and hiring other virtual assistants to work for you can generate passive income.

5. YouTube videos: Creating YouTube videos and monetizing them through ads, sponsorships, and affiliate marketing can generate passive income.

6. Podcasting: Creating a podcast and monetizing it through sponsorships and affiliate marketing can generate passive income.

7. App development: Developing and selling mobile apps on the App Store or Google Play can generate passive income.

8. Online marketplaces: Setting up an online marketplace and earning a commission on sales or rental fees can generate passive income.

9. Bond laddering: Investing in bonds with different maturity dates can provide a steady stream of passive income as the bonds mature and pay interest.

10. Robo-advisors: Investing in robo-advisors like Betterment and Wealthfront can provide a hands-off way to generate passive income through a diversified portfolio of low-cost index funds.

11. Self-storage: Investing in self-storage facilities can provide passive income through rental income from tenants.

12. Income producing websites: Setting up and monetizing a website through advertising, affiliate marketing, or sponsored content can generate passive income.

13. Virtual real estate: Investing in virtual real estate like websites, domain names, and online businesses can generate passive income through advertising, affiliate marketing, and sponsorships.

14. Blogging: Setting up a blog and monetizing it through advertising, affiliate marketing, sponsored posts, and e-commerce can generate passive income.

15. Gaming: Investing in video games and virtual assets can generate passive income through sales and rentals.

16. Photography: Investing in photography and licensing your images through stock photography websites can generate passive income.

17. Subscription boxes: Setting up a subscription box business and sourcing products from vendors can generate passive income.

18. Online marketplaces: Setting up an online marketplace and earning a commission on sales or rental fees can generate passive income.

19. Investing in a franchise: Investing in a franchise can provide passive income through royalties and a percentage of sales.

20. Investing in a business: Investing in a business can provide passive income through dividends or a percentage of profits.

It's important to remember that while these methods can provide passive income, they still require effort and time to set up and maintain. Additionally, some methods may require initial investments and may not be suitable for everyone. It's always important to do research and understand the risks and potential returns of any investment or business before committing. In conclusion, there are many different ways to generate passive income, each with its own unique set of benefits and challenges. The key to generating passive income is to find a method that aligns with your interests and skills and to invest the time and resources necessary to make it a success. With the right approach and mindset, anyone can generate passive income and achieve financial freedom and security.

Second Income

Generating a second income is a great way to boost your overall financial security and help you achieve your financial goals. There are many ways to earn a second income, and one effective strategy is to take on multiple professions. This can involve working a part-time or freelance job, starting a small business, or renting out a spare room on Airbnb.

One way to generate a second income is to take on a part-time or freelance job. This could be something as simple as working a few hours a week at a retail store or restaurant, or something more specialized like writing, graphic design or programming. Many people find that working a part-time or freelance job can be a great way to earn extra money, and it can also provide valuable skills and experience that can be used to further your career.

Another way to generate a second income is to start a small business. This could be something as simple as starting a lawn care service or dog-walking business, or something more complex like launching an e-commerce website or developing a mobile app. Starting a small business can be a great way to earn extra money and gain valuable skills and experience.

Renting out a spare room on Airbnb is another way to generate a second income. This can be a great way to earn extra money by renting out a spare room in your home or apartment to travelers. This can be a great way to earn extra money, and it can also be a fun and interesting way to meet new people.

Investing in dividend paying stocks or mutual funds can be a great way to generate a second income. Dividends are payments made to shareholders of a company and it can provide a steady stream of income without having to sell shares. It's important to research the company and the dividends they are paying out before investing.

Another way to generate a second income is to become an affiliate marketer. This involves promoting other people's products or services and earning a commission on any sales made through your affiliate link. Affiliate marketing can be done through a blog, website, or social media and it can be done part-time.

In summary, there are many ways to generate a second income, and one effective strategy is to take on multiple professions. This can include working a part-time or freelance job, starting a small business, renting out a spare room on Airbnb, Investing in dividend paying stocks or mutual funds or becoming an affiliate marketer. Each of these options has the potential to provide a steady stream of additional income and can help you achieve your financial goals. It's important to consider your skills, interests and the amount of time you are willing to commit to generating a second income before making a decision.

Chapter 9

Investment in Stock Market

Investment is when you put your money into something with the expectation of making more money in the future. It's like planting a seed, you put in money now and wait for it to grow. But not all opportunities to invest money are good. So, before you invest, you have to do your research and make sure it's a safe and smart investment.

In his book "The Intelligent Investor," Benjamin Graham defines investment as "an operation which, upon thorough analysis promises safety of principal and an adequate return. Operations not meeting these requirements are speculative."

In other words, according to Graham, an investment is a deliberate commitment of resources (such as money or time) to a particular endeavor, with the expectation of obtaining a satisfactory return while maintaining the safety of the initial investment. He emphasizes the importance of thorough analysis and due diligence in determining whether an opportunity is truly an investment or a speculative venture.

Graham's definition highlights the difference between investing and speculating, where investing is a deliberate decision made after thorough research and analysis, while speculating is more of a gamble, and usually not backed by proper analysis.

One of the most common forms of investment is buying stocks in a publicly traded company. When an individual buys shares of stock, they are essentially buying a small piece of ownership in the company. If the company performs well and its stock price increases, the individual's investment will also increase in value. However, if the company performs poorly and its stock price decreases, the individual's investment will also decrease in value.

Another popular form of investment is real estate. This can include buying property to rent out to tenants, flipping houses for a profit, or investing in a real estate investment trust (REIT). Real estate investments can be a great way to generate passive income, as well as build wealth over time through appreciation of the property's value.

Investing in precious metals, such as gold and silver, can also be a way to diversify an investment portfolio and potentially protect against inflation. Precious metals have historically held value over time and can act as a hedge against economic uncertainty.

Overall, investment is a way for individuals and organizations to grow their wealth over time by committing money or capital to an asset with the expectation of obtaining an additional income or profit. It is important to keep in mind that while investing can be a great way to build wealth, it also comes with risk. It is essential to do thorough research and consider the potential risks and rewards before making any investment decisions.

It is also important to diversify investment portfolios across different asset class, sectors, geographies and time horizon. This will help to mitigate the risk and maximize the returns. Additionally, it is also important to have a long-term perspective and avoid chasing hot investments or trying to time the market.

In summary, Investment is a powerful tool for growing and preserving wealth, but it's important to approach it with a long-term perspective, diversify investments, and carefully consider the potential risks and rewards before making any investment decisions.

Long Term Investing Vs Short Term Speculation

When it comes to investing, there are two main approaches: long-term investing and short-term speculation. Long-term investing involves committing money or capital to an asset with the expectation of holding it for an extended period of time, typically several years or more. Short-term speculation, on the other hand, involves making quick, high-risk investments with the expectation of selling the asset in a relatively short period of time, such as a few months or less.

While short-term speculation can sometimes lead to quick profits, it is important to understand the potential risks and downsides of this approach. One of the biggest risks of short-term speculation is the potential for significant losses. When the goal is to make a quick profit, investors may not take the time to thoroughly research an investment opportunity and may end up losing a significant amount of money. Additionally, short-term speculation can be quite volatile and unpredictable, making it a risky strategy for those who are not experienced or are not willing to take on high levels of risk.

One of the main reasons why short-term speculation cannot be scaled is because it is based on market timing. In order to make a profit through short-term speculation, investors must correctly predict the direction of the market and the timing of when to buy and sell an asset. This is a difficult task, even for experienced investors, and it is nearly impossible to consistently predict the market over an extended period of time.

Another reason why short-term speculation cannot be scaled is because it is based on high-risk, high-reward investments. These types of investments are not suitable for most investors and can lead to significant losses if the investment does not perform as expected. Additionally, the high-risk nature of short-term speculation makes it difficult to consistently make profits over an extended period of time, as a few bad investments can wipe out any gains made through previous investments.

Furthermore, Short-term speculation is also affected by a high level of volatility, as the market fluctuates frequently, so the investor who intends to hold the asset for a short period of time will have to pay a higher fee and may face more significant losses in the event of a market downturn.

On the other hand, long-term investing offers a number of benefits. One of the main advantages of long-term investing is the potential for compound growth. When an investment is held for an extended period of time, the returns on that investment can compound, leading to significant growth in the value of the investment. Additionally, long-term investing allows investors to ride out market fluctuations and avoid the temptation to make impulsive decisions based on short-term market movements.

Another advantage of long-term investing is that it allows investors to focus on the fundamentals of a company or an asset. Instead of trying to time the market or chasing short-term gains, long-term investors can focus on the underlying value of a company or asset, such as its earnings, revenue, and growth potential. This can help investors make more informed decisions and avoid the pitfalls of short-term speculation.

In addition, long-term investing helps to mitigate the risk by diversifying the portfolio across different asset class, sectors, geographies and time horizon. This helps to ensure that a portfolio is not overly exposed to any one particular risk and can withstand market fluctuations.

Overall, while short-term speculation can sometimes lead to quick profits, it is a high-risk strategy that is not suitable for most investors. Long-term investing, on the other hand, offers a number of benefits, including the potential for compound growth, the ability to ride out market fluctuations, and the ability to focus on the fundamentals of a company or asset. For these reasons, long-term investing is generally considered to be a more sound and reliable approach to building wealth over time.

In summary, Long-term investing is a strategy that focuses on committing money or capital to an asset with the expectation of holding it for an extended period of time, typically several years or more, while short-term speculation is a strategy that involves making quick, high-risk investments with the expectation of selling the asset in a relatively short period of time. Long-term investing offers many benefits over short-term speculation, such as the potential for compound growth, the ability to ride out market fluctuations, the ability to focus on the fundamentals of a company or asset, and the ability to diversify portfolio, which makes it a more sound and reliable approach to building wealth over time.

Understanding Equity

Equity, also known as stocks or shares, represents ownership in a company. When you invest in equity, you are buying shares in a company and becoming a shareholder. As a shareholder, you are entitled to a portion of the company's profits and assets, and you have the potential to earn a return on your investment through capital appreciation or dividends.

When investing in equity, it's important to understand that the value of your investment can be affected by a wide range of factors, including the company's financial performance, the overall health of the economy, and market conditions. Additionally, equity investments are generally considered to be more risky than debt investments, but they also have the potential for higher returns. It's always recommended to consult with a financial advisor before making any investment decisions, and diversify your investments across different sectors and companies to minimize the risk.

Stock Exchanges: Nasdaq, NYSE, NSE, BSE

Stock exchanges are organizations that provide a platform for buying and selling stocks, bonds, and other securities. Some of the most well-known stock exchanges in the world include the Nasdaq, the New York Stock Exchange (NYSE), the National Stock Exchange of India (NSE), and the Bombay Stock Exchange (BSE).

Nasdaq

Nasdaq is an American stock exchange that was founded in 1971. It is known for being the first electronic stock market, and it is the second-largest stock exchange in the world by market capitalization. Nasdaq lists a wide variety of companies, including technology, biotech, and consumer goods companies. Some well-known companies listed on Nasdaq include Apple, Amazon, and Netflix.

NYSE

The New York Stock Exchange (NYSE) is the largest stock exchange in the world by market capitalization. It was founded in 1792 and is located in New York City. The NYSE lists a wide variety of companies, including blue-chip companies, and it is known for its strict listing requirements. Some well-known companies listed on the NYSE include Coca-Cola, General Electric, and IBM.

NSE

The National Stock Exchange of India (NSE) is the largest stock exchange in India by market capitalization. It was established in 1992 and is headquartered in Mumbai. The NSE offers a wide range of products and services, including equities, derivatives, and debt instruments. Some well-known companies listed on the NSE include Reliance Industries, Tata Consultancy Services, and HDFC Bank.

BSE

The Bombay Stock Exchange (BSE) is the oldest stock exchange in Asia, established in 1875. It is located in Mumbai, India. BSE has been the first exchange in the world to obtain an ISO 9001:2000 certification. It offers a wide range of products and services, including equities, derivatives, and debt instruments. Some well-known companies listed on the BSE include State Bank of India, Tata Motors, and Wipro.

Stock exchanges play a crucial role in the functioning of capital markets by providing a transparent and regulated platform for buying and selling securities. They also provide a mechanism for companies to raise capital by issuing shares to the public. Additionally, stock exchanges provide investors with an opportunity to invest in a variety of companies and sectors, and to participate in the growth of the economy.

Indices: Nasdaq, S&P 500, Dow Jones, Sensex and Nifty

An index is a statistical measure of the performance of a group of stocks or other securities. Indices are used to track the performance of a particular market or sector and are often used as a benchmark for the performance of a portfolio or mutual fund. Some of the most well-known indices include the Nasdaq, the S&P 500, the Dow Jones Industrial Average, the Sensex, and the Nifty.

Nasdaq

The Nasdaq Composite Index is an index of the top 100 stocks that are listed on the Nasdaq stock exchange. The index is designed to represent the performance of the technology-heavy Nasdaq market and includes companies such as Apple, Amazon, and Microsoft.

S&P 500

The S&P 500 Index is a market capitalization-weighted index that comprises of 500 of the largest publicly traded companies in the United States. The index is considered a benchmark for the US stock market and includes companies such as Apple, Microsoft, and Amazon.

Dow Jones Industrial Average

The Dow Jones Industrial Average (DJIA) is an index of 30 blue-chip stocks that are listed on the New York Stock Exchange. The DJIA is considered a benchmark for the US stock market and includes companies such as Boeing, Coca-Cola, and IBM.

Sensex

The Sensex, also known as the BSE 30, is an index of 30 of the largest publicly traded companies in India that are listed on the Bombay Stock Exchange. The Sensex is considered a benchmark for the Indian stock market and includes companies such as Reliance Industries, Tata Consultancy Services, and HDFC Bank.

Nifty

The Nifty 50 is an index of 50 of the largest publicly traded companies in India that are listed on the National Stock Exchange of India. The Nifty 50 is considered a benchmark for the Indian stock market and includes companies such as HDFC Bank, Reliance Industries and Tata Consultancy Services.

Indices can be used as a benchmark for performance, for investment decisions and as a tool to measure the overall health of a market or sector. They also provide a way for investors to track the performance of a particular market or sector without having to buy individual stocks.

Types of Equity Investments

There are several different types of equity investments that individuals can make, each with their own set of pros and cons. Some of the most common types include:

Direct Stock Investment

This type of investment involves buying shares of individual stocks on the stock exchange. This can be done through a brokerage account, and investors are able to buy and sell shares as they wish. The main advantage of direct stock investment is that it allows investors to have complete control over their portfolio and the ability to make quick decisions based on market conditions. However, it also carries a high level of risk as the performance of an individual stock is more volatile than a diversified portfolio.

Active Mutual Fund Investment

Active mutual funds are managed by a professional fund manager who actively chooses which stocks to include in the fund. These funds typically have higher fees than index funds because of the added cost of the fund manager's expertise. However, active funds have the potential to outperform index funds if the fund manager is skilled in selecting winning stocks.

Index Fund Investment

Index funds are mutual funds that are designed to mimic the performance of a particular stock market index. They are passively managed and therefore have lower expense ratios than active funds. Index funds provide a low-cost way to achieve diversification and to track the performance of a particular market or sector, but they will not outperform the market.

Exchange Traded Funds (ETFs)

ETFs are similar to index funds but they trade on the stock exchange like a stock. They are a basket of securities that track an index, commodity or a basket of assets, like an index fund but can be traded on an exchange throughout the trading day. ETFs can be used as a low-cost, efficient way to gain exposure to a specific sector or market, and they also provide liquidity as they can be bought and sold at any time during trading hours.

Hedge Funds

Hedge funds are a type of investment vehicle that are typically available only to high-net-worth individuals and institutional investors. They are known for their use of unconventional investment strategies, such as short selling, leverage, and derivatives. Hedge funds are typically run by professional money managers, who have significant experience and expertise in the financial markets. These managers have significant discretion over the investment decisions and have the freedom to invest in a wide range of assets, including stocks, bonds, currencies, commodities, and derivatives.

Portfolio Management Services

PMS or Portfolio Management Services refer to a type of investment service offered by asset management companies where a team of professional portfolio managers manage and invest the funds of high-net-worth individuals, family offices, trusts and other institutional investors. In PMS, the investors give discretionary powers to the portfolio manager to take investment decisions on their behalf. The portfolio manager then creates and manages a portfolio of stocks, bonds, mutual funds, and other securities that align with the investor's financial goals and risk tolerance.

Real Estate Investment Trust (REITs)

REITs are companies that own and operate income-producing real estate, such as apartments, office buildings, and shopping centers. They are traded on the stock exchange and provide investors with a way to gain exposure to the real estate market without having to directly own property. REITs pay out a large portion of their income as dividends, which can provide a steady stream of income for investors.

Each type of equity investment has its own set of advantages and disadvantages, and the best option for an individual investor will depend on their investment goals, risk tolerance, and overall financial situation.

Advantages of Index Funds over Active Mutual Funds/Hedge Funds

Index fund investing is considered to be a better option than active mutual fund investing for a few reasons:

Lower Costs: Index funds typically have lower expense ratios than actively managed funds. This is because index funds simply track a specific market index, so they don't need to pay for research and analysis to pick individual stocks.

Better Performance: Over the long term, index funds have been shown to perform better than actively managed funds. This is because it's difficult for active fund managers to consistently beat the market, and many active funds underperform their benchmark indices.

Tax Efficiency: Index funds tend to be more tax-efficient than actively managed funds. This is because index funds have lower turnover, which means they don't need to sell as many securities to generate returns. This means that index funds generate fewer capital gains, which can lead to lower taxes.

Simplicity: Index funds are generally considered to be simpler than actively managed funds. This is because they simply track a specific market index, so investors don't need to spend time researching individual stocks. Additionally, because index funds are diversified, they provide investors with broad market exposure, which reduces the need for investors to actively manage their portfolio.

Lower risk: Because index funds track a market index, they're diversified by default. This diversification can help lower risk in the portfolio. Actively managed funds, on the other hand, are often concentrated in a particular sector or style, which can increase risk.

It's important to note that index funds aren't without risks and investors should diversify their portfolio and have a long-term investment horizon. Additionally, index funds may not be suitable for all investors, especially for those with a high-risk tolerance and looking for higher returns over a short period of time.

Warren Buffet on Index Funds and Efficient Market Hypothesis

Warren Buffett, one of the most successful investors of all time, is a proponent of index fund investing. He believes that it's difficult for active investors to consistently beat the market, and that most investors are better off investing in index funds rather than trying to pick individual stocks.

In his annual letter to Berkshire Hathaway shareholders in 2018, Buffett wrote, "When trillions of dollars are managed by Wall Streeters charging high fees, it will usually be the managers who reap outsized profits, not the clients. Both large and small investors should stick with low-cost index funds."

Buffett's endorsement of index funds aligns with the efficient market hypothesis (EMH), which states that markets are efficient and that it's difficult for investors to consistently achieve returns above the market average. EMH argues that the stock prices of publicly traded companies reflect all publicly available information, and that it's impossible to consistently buy undervalued stocks or sell overvalued ones.

Buffett's view is that most investors can't beat the market, and that it's better to simply invest in a low-cost index fund that tracks a broad market index like the S&P 500. He argues that by doing so, investors will earn returns that are similar to the overall market, which are likely to be better than the returns earned by most active investors.

It's worth noting that while Buffett is a proponent of index funds, he is also a value investor and has been able to achieve returns above the market average over the long term. However, he is aware that most investors don't have the skill set, resources or time to do what he does, and that's why he advocates for index funds.

Warren Buffet's Million Dollar Bet

In 2007, Warren Buffett made a $1 million bet that a passively managed fund indexed to the S&P 500 would outperform a selection of hedge funds over the course of a decade. The bet was against Protégé Partners, a firm that ran a fund of hedge funds.

The bet began on January 1, 2008 and ended on December 31, 2017. At the end of the bet, the S&P 500 index fund returned 7.1% per year, while the hedge funds returned an average of 2.2% per year. The bet was settled in Buffett's favor, and he donated the winnings to charity.

Buffett's bet was a way to make a point about the high fees and underperformance of many hedge funds. He argued that most investors would be better off investing in a low-cost index fund rather than paying the high fees associated with hedge funds. He also argued that it's difficult for active managers to consistently outperform the market over the long term.

The bet also highlighted the importance of keeping investment costs low and investing in a diversified portfolio of low-cost index funds. This approach can increase the chances of earning returns that are similar to the overall market, which is likely to be better than the returns earned by most active investors.

Any Monkey Can Beat the Market

The phrase "any monkey can beat the market" is often used to highlight the idea that investing in the stock market is not as difficult as some people may think. The phrase is used to make the point that even a monkey, with no knowledge or understanding of the stock market, could potentially beat the market by randomly picking stocks.

The idea behind this phrase is that the stock market is efficient, meaning that all publicly available information is already reflected in the current stock prices. Therefore, it is unlikely that an individual investor or even professional fund manager will consistently outperform the market, as they will not have access to any new information that the market does not already know.

Additionally, it's also hard for an individual to have enough information and resources to make informed investment decisions, as well as the time and expertise to effectively manage a portfolio of securities.

Warren Buffett, one of the most successful investors of all time, has famously said that "The best thing a person can do for his financial health is to minimize his expenditures. Let the market do the work." He has also advocated for index fund investing, which is a passive investment strategy where an investor buys a basket of securities that represent a market index, such as the S&P 500.

In conclusion, while it may be possible for some investors to beat the market, it is difficult for most investors to consistently outperform the market over time. Many experts recommend a passive investment strategy such as index fund investing as a more efficient and less time-consuming way to invest.

Survivorship Bias

Survivorship bias is a phenomenon that occurs when mutual funds that have performed poorly are removed or "survive" out of the mutual fund universe and are not included in the performance data. This can lead to the false impression that active mutual funds as a whole have performed better than they actually have.

When it comes to comparing index fund investing to active mutual fund investing, survivorship bias can create a skewed picture of the performance of active mutual funds. This is because mutual funds that underperform are more likely to be closed or merged with other funds. As a result, the performance data for active mutual funds does not include the poor-performing funds, making the group as a whole appear to have performed better than it actually has.

On the other hand, index funds simply track a specific market index, such as the S&P 500, and are not subject to survivorship bias. Because index funds hold all the securities in the index regardless of their performance, investors can be sure they are getting a true representation of the market's performance.

Another advantage of index fund investing is the low cost. Index funds have lower expenses as they don't require expensive research teams or analysts to pick securities.

In conclusion, survivorship bias can make active mutual funds appear to have performed better than they actually have, and index funds provide a true representation of the market's performance and are a cost-effective way to invest.

SIP Vs Lumpsum

SIP (Systematic Investment Plan) and lump-sum investment are both methods of investing, but they differ in the way they allow investors to invest their money.

Lump-sum investment refers to the practice of investing a large amount of money all at once, usually in a single transaction. This method of investing is best suited for individuals who have a large amount of money available to invest and are comfortable with market fluctuations.

On the other hand, SIP is a method of investing a fixed amount of money at regular intervals, such as weekly, monthly, or quarterly, in a mutual fund or other investment vehicle. The idea behind an SIP is to make it easy for investors to invest small amounts of money on a regular basis without having to time the market or make large lump-sum investments.

One of the main advantages of SIP is that it allows investors to invest a small amount of money regularly over a period of time, rather than investing a large sum of money all at once. This makes it an ideal investment option for individuals who do not have a large amount of money to invest at one time.

SIP also helps investors to reduce the risk of investing in the market. When an investor invests a large sum of money all at once, the investment is vulnerable to market fluctuations. With SIP, the investor is investing small amounts of money at regular intervals, which helps to average out the cost of the investment. This is known as rupee cost averaging.

Another advantage of SIP is that it allows investors to invest in mutual funds or other investment vehicles at a lower cost. Many mutual funds offer discounts or other incentives to investors who participate in an SIP.

On the other hand, lump-sum investment may be more beneficial when markets are low and are expected to rise. This is because the investor is able to buy more units of the mutual fund or other investment vehicle when the price is low.

In conclusion, both SIP and lump-sum investment have their own advantages and disadvantages. SIP is best suited for individuals who want to invest small amounts of money regularly, while lump-sum investment is best suited for individuals who have a large amount of money to invest all at once and are comfortable with market fluctuations. The choice between SIP and lump-sum investment depends on an individual's investment goals, risk tolerance, and financial situation.

Risks Associated with Equity Investments

Equity investments, also known as stock investments, come with a certain level of risk. Here are some of the main risks associated with equity investments:

Market Risk: The value of equity investments can fluctuate due to changes in the overall stock market. When the stock market is performing well, the value of equity investments will generally increase. However, when the market is performing poorly, the value of equity investments will decrease. This risk is present for all equity investments, regardless of the specific company or sector.

Company-Specific Risk: Equity investments in a specific company come with the risk that the company may not perform as well as expected. This can be due to a variety of factors such as poor management, increased competition, or a decline in the industry as a whole.

Interest Rate Risk: Interest rate risk refers to the impact that changes in interest rates can have on the value of equity investments. When interest rates rise, bond prices fall, and bond yields rise, which can lead to a decline in the value of equity investments.

Political and Economic Risk: Equity investments can be affected by political and economic events such as wars, natural disasters, and changes in government policies. These events can have a negative impact on a company's performance, which can lead to a decline in the value of equity investments.

Liquidity Risk: Liquidity risk refers to the difficulty in selling an equity investment quickly and at a fair price. Some companies may have few market participants, and therefore, it may be difficult to find a buyer for an equity investment.

It's important to understand these risks before investing in equity. Diversifying the portfolio and investing in different sectors, geographies and companies can help mitigate the risks. Additionally, investors should have a long-term investment horizon and should be comfortable with the volatility that comes with equity investments.

Direct Stock Investments

Direct stock investment, also known as individual stock investing, is the process of purchasing and holding stocks in individual companies. This can be done by purchasing shares of stock directly through a brokerage account or through a direct stock purchase plan offered by the company.

Pros of Direct Stock Investment:

Potential for high returns: By investing in individual stocks, investors have the potential to earn higher returns than they would with a more diversified investment such as a mutual fund.

Control over investment choices: When investing in individual stocks, investors have more control over the companies in which they are investing and can make investment decisions based on their own research and analysis.

Flexibility: Individual stocks can be bought or sold at any time, giving investors the flexibility to make quick decisions based on market conditions or personal financial needs.

Cons of Direct Stock Investment

Higher risk: Investing in individual stocks can be riskier than investing in a diversified portfolio of stocks because the performance of a single stock is closely tied to the performance of the specific company.

Time-consuming: Investing in individual stocks requires a significant amount of research and analysis in order to make informed investment decisions. This can be time-consuming and may not be feasible for all investors.

Lack of diversification: Investing in individual stocks can lead to a lack of diversification in a portfolio, which can increase overall risk.

In summary, Direct stock investment can offer the potential for high returns, but it is generally considered to be a higher-risk investment strategy. It is important for investors to conduct thorough research and analysis before investing in individual stocks and to maintain a diversified portfolio.

Fundamental Stock Analysis

Fundamental stock analysis is a method of evaluating a company's financial and economic fundamentals in order to determine its intrinsic value and potential for future growth. This type of analysis looks at factors such as the company's revenue, earnings, assets, liabilities, and management team, as well as its industry and market conditions.

Grade A Moats

One key aspect of fundamental stock analysis is the concept of a "economic moat" or "competitive advantage". The term moat, popularized by Warren Buffett, refers to a company's ability to maintain a sustainable competitive advantage over its rivals. A company with a wide moat is considered to have a stronger ability to withstand competition and generate consistent profits over time.

One way to identify a company with a wide moat is to look for the presence of "Grade A Moats". These are characteristics that give a company a sustainable competitive advantage in its industry, such as:

Low cost product: A company that can produce and sell products at a lower cost than its competitors has a significant advantage in the market.

Brand Value: A strong brand can be a powerful competitive advantage as it can help a company to charge premium prices and increase customer loyalty.

Low cost of R&D: A company that can keep its research and development costs low has a significant advantage in terms of innovation and product development.

Large Distribution network: A company with a large distribution network can reach more customers and quickly respond to market changes.

Taste: A company with a unique taste or recipe that is hard to replicate by its competitors.

One example of a company that has a wide moat and grade A moats is Coca-Cola. Coca-Cola's brand value is one of the strongest in the world, and it has a wide distribution network that allows it to reach customers in more than 200 countries. Additionally, its secret recipe for the coke is considered a trade secret and is hard to replicate. Furthermore, it has a large distribution network that allows it to quickly respond to market changes and reach a wide range of customers. All of these factors help Coca-Cola to maintain a sustainable competitive advantage in the market and generate consistent profits over time.

Grade B Moats

Grade B moats refer to companies that have a sustainable competitive advantage, but not as strong as a grade A moats. These companies may not have a wide economic moat and may be vulnerable to competition in the long term.

For example, a company that specializes in low cost product would be a good example of a grade B moat. The company may have a strong distribution network, brand value, and low cost of R&D. However, they may not have a wide economic moat or a taste which is hard to replicate.

One example of such company is Walmart, It has a strong distribution network, brand value, and low-cost structure. However, it is vulnerable to competition from online retailers like Amazon, and its growth prospects may be limited in the long term.

Grade C Moats

Grade C moats refer to companies that have a limited or no sustainable competitive advantage. These companies may have strong financials and good management, but they are vulnerable to competition and may have limited growth prospects.

For example, a retail company that operates in a highly competitive market with several similar players and where customers have little brand loyalty would be a good example of a company with a grade C moat.

One example of such company is department store chain such as J.C. Penney, which has struggled in recent years as competition from online retailers and discount stores has increased. The company has struggled to differentiate itself from its competitors and has been unable to build a sustainable competitive advantage. As a result, the company has seen its sales and profits decline, and it has been forced to close stores.

Balance Sheet of a Company

A balance sheet is a financial statement that shows a company's assets, liabilities, and equity at a specific point in time. It is used to understand the financial health and stability of a company. The balance sheet is divided into two sections: assets and liabilities + equity.

Assets:

Current assets: These are assets that can be converted into cash within one year, such as cash and cash equivalents, accounts receivable, and inventory.

Non-current assets: These are assets that cannot be converted into cash within one year, such as property, plant, and equipment, intangible assets, and investments.

Liabilities:

Current liabilities: These are liabilities that must be paid within one year, such as accounts payable, short-term debt, and taxes payable.

Non-current liabilities: These are liabilities that are not due within one year, such as long-term debt and pension liabilities.

Equity:

Shareholders' equity: This section includes the company's common stock, retained earnings, and any other equity accounts.

It is important to note that assets must equal liabilities + equity, as per the accounting equation: Assets = Liabilities + Equity

An example of balance sheet of a company is as follows:

Assets:

Current assets: $5,000 (cash and cash equivalents), $10,000 (accounts receivable), $15,000 (inventory)

Non-current assets: $50,000 (property, plant, and equipment), $20,000 (intangible assets), $10,000 (investments)

Liabilities:

Current liabilities: $10,000 (accounts payable), $5,000 (short-term debt), $2,500 (taxes payable)

Non-current liabilities: $30,000 (long-term debt), $5,000 (pension liabilities)

Equity:

Shareholders' equity: $35,000 (common stock), $15,000 (retained earnings)

Total assets: $100,000 Total liabilities + equity: $100,000

By reading the balance sheet, an investor can get a sense of the company's liquidity (how easily assets can be converted into cash), its debt levels, and its shareholders' equity. This information can be used to assess the company's overall financial health and to make informed investment decisions.

Income Statement of a Company

The income statement, also known as the profit and loss statement, shows a company's revenues, expenses, and profits over a period of time, typically a quarter or a year.

Sales, revenue, turnover, and topline all refer to the amount of money a company brings in through its operations. For example, if a company sells $100,000 worth of goods or services, that would be its topline.

Cost of goods sold (COGS) includes the direct costs associated with producing and selling a product or service. For example, if a company sells $100,000 worth of goods and the cost of producing those goods was $60,000, then its COGS is $60,000.

Gross profit is calculated by subtracting the COGS from the topline. In the example above, the gross profit would be $40,000 ($100,000 - $60,000).

Operating expenses (SG&A) are the costs a company incurs that are not directly related to producing and selling a product or service. These expenses include things like selling, general, and administrative expenses. For example, if a company has operating expenses of $20,000, then its operating profit (EBIT) would be $20,000 ($40,000 - $20,000).

Depreciation and amortization are non-cash expenses that represent the cost of using an asset over time. These expenses are subtracted from operating profit to arrive at the profit before tax (PBT).

Interest is the cost of borrowing money and is also subtracted from operating profit to arrive at the PBT.

Profit before tax (PBT) is then adjusted for taxes to arrive at the net income (NI/PAT/Bottomline/Net profit).

For example, let's take a company XYZ. If it has $1000000 as sales, $700000 as cost of goods sold, $300000 as operating expenses and $100000 as depreciation and amortization, $50000 as interest expense, $200000 as tax. then its gross profit would be $300000 (1000000-700000), operating profit (EBIT) would be $100000 (300000-200000), PBT would be $50000 (100000-50000) and Net Income would be $30000 (50000-20000)

It's important to understand the income statement and balance sheet to get a sense of a company's financial health and performance. With the help of these statements, investors can analyze a company's revenue and expenses, as well as its assets and liabilities, to make informed investment decisions.

Understanding Key Financial Ratios

P/E ratio (Price-to-Earnings ratio)

P/E ratio (Price-to-Earnings ratio) is a valuation ratio that compares the market price of a stock to its earnings per share (EPS). It is calculated by dividing the market price of a stock by its EPS. A lower P/E ratio indicates that the stock is cheaper when compared to a stock with a higher P/E ratio.

PEG ratio (Price-to-Earnings-to-Growth ratio)

PEG ratio (Price-to-Earnings-to-Growth ratio) is a valuation ratio that compares the P/E ratio of a stock to its growth rate. It is calculated by dividing the P/E ratio by the annual earnings growth rate. A lower PEG ratio indicates that a stock is undervalued when compared to a stock with a higher PEG ratio.

P/B ratio (Price-to-Book ratio)

P/B ratio (Price-to-Book ratio) is a valuation ratio that compares the market price of a stock to its book value. It is calculated by dividing the market price of a stock by its book value per share. A lower P/B ratio indicates that a stock is undervalued when compared to a stock with a higher P/B ratio.

D/E ratio (Debt-to-Equity ratio)

D/E ratio (Debt-to-Equity ratio) is a financial leverage ratio that compares a company's total debt to its total equity. It is calculated by dividing the total debt of a company by its total equity. A higher D/E ratio indicates that a company is more leveraged and is more risky when compared to a company with a lower D/E ratio.

Gross Profit Margin

Gross Profit Margin is a profitability ratio that compares a company's gross profit to its revenue. It is calculated by dividing the gross profit by the revenue. A higher gross profit margin indicates that a company is more profitable when compared to a company with a lower gross profit margin.

Operating Profit Margin

Operating Profit Margin is a profitability ratio that compares a company's operating profit to its revenue. It is calculated by dividing the operating profit by the revenue. A higher operating profit margin indicates that a company is more profitable when compared to a company with a lower operating profit margin.

Interest Coverage Ratio

Interest Coverage Ratio is a financial leverage ratio that compares a company's earnings before interest and taxes to its interest expense. It is calculated by dividing the earnings before interest and taxes by the interest expense. A higher interest coverage ratio indicates that a company is more capable of meeting its interest obligations when compared to a company with a lower interest coverage ratio.

ROE (Return on Equity)

ROE (Return on Equity) is a profitability ratio that compares a company's net income to its shareholder's equity. It is calculated by dividing the net income by the shareholder's equity. A higher return on equity indicates that a company is more profitable when compared to a company with a lower return on equity.

Free cash flow

Free cash flow is the cash that a company generates after accounting for capital expenditures. It is important because it allows a company to pursue opportunities that enhance shareholder value. A positive free cash flow is an indication that a company's business is healthy and generating cash.

Example: Let's take the example of Coca-Cola (KO). The P/E ratio of Coca-Cola is 27.33, PEG ratio is 3.20, P/B ratio is 7.44, D/E ratio is 0.57, Gross Profit Margin is 60.21%, Operating Profit Margin is 27.17%, Interest Coverage Ratio is 8.41, Return on Equity is 34.11% and Free Cash Flow is $8.04 billion.

Technical Stock Analysis

Technical stock analysis is a method of evaluating securities by analyzing statistics generated by market activity, such as past prices and volume. Technical analysts believe that the historical performance of a stock, along with various other market and economic indicators, can be used to predict its future performance.

One example of a technical analysis indicator is the moving average. A moving average is a calculation of the average price of a security over a specified number of periods. A 50-day moving average, for example, would be the average price of a stock over the past 50 days. A simple moving average (SMA) is a moving average that is calculated by adding the closing price of a stock for a number of time periods and then dividing this total by the number of time periods.

Another example of a technical analysis indicator is the relative strength index (RSI). The RSI is a momentum indicator that compares the magnitude of recent gains to recent losses in an attempt to determine overbought and oversold conditions of an asset. The RSI ranges from 0 to 100, and traditional interpretation and usage of the RSI is that RSI values of 70 or above indicate that a stock is overbought or overvalued, and therefore may be primed for a trend reversal or corrective pullback in price.

It's worth noting that Technical Analysis is generally used in conjunction with Fundamental Analysis as Technical Analysis is based on past performance of stock prices, while fundamental analysis is based on the underlying financial and economic factors that can affect the stock price.

How to Calculate the Stock Price of a Company

Up until now, we have been focused on using fundamental analysis to determine what stocks to purchase. This process involves analyzing a company's financial and operational performance to determine its intrinsic value. However, simply knowing what stock to buy is not enough. In order to maximize our returns, we also need to know when to buy that stock. This is where technical analysis comes in. Technical analysis is the process of evaluating a stock's price and volume data to identify patterns and trends that can be used to predict future price movements. One important aspect of technical analysis is calculating the price of a stock, which involves analyzing factors such as support and resistance levels, moving averages, and relative strength indicators. By combining both fundamental and technical analysis, we can make more informed decisions about when to buy and sell stocks to maximize our returns.

Discounted Cash Flow (DCF) Analysis

Discounted Cash Flow (DCF) Analysis is a method of valuing a company by estimating the future cash flows it is expected to generate and discounting them to present value. The basic idea behind the DCF method is that the value of an investment is equal to the sum of all its future cash flows, discounted at an appropriate rate.

To illustrate how the DCF method works, let's take the example of a company XYZ. Assume that the company is expected to generate cash flows of $10 million in year 1, $12 million in year 2, $15 million in year 3, and $20 million in year 4. The company's cost of capital (discount rate) is assumed to be 10%.

The first step in the DCF analysis is to estimate the future cash flows. In this case, the future cash flows are estimated to be $10 million in year 1, $12 million in year 2, $15 million in year 3, and $20 million in year 4.

The next step is to discount these future cash flows to present value. This is done by dividing each future cash flow by (1+discount rate) raised to the power of the year in which the cash flow is expected. For example, the present value of the cash flow of $10 million in year 1 is $10 million / $(1+0.1)^1$ = $9.09 million. Similarly, the present value of the cash flow of $12 million in year 2 is $12 million / (1+0.1)^2 = $10.38 million.

Finally, we add up all the present values of the future cash flows to get the intrinsic value of the company. In this case, the intrinsic value of the company XYZ is $9.09 million + $10.38 million + $12.50 million + $15.87 million = $47.84 million. When we divide this value from the total number of stocks available in the market for this company, we can calculate the stock price of the company.

It's worth noting that the DCF method is a forward-looking technique and it requires a number of assumptions about future growth rates, interest rates, and other factors. Therefore, it's important to be cautious when interpreting the results of a DCF analysis and consider other factors as well such as industry trends, economic conditions, and management quality when evaluating a company.

Using Options Strategies for Stock Hedging

Options are financial contracts that give the holder the right, but not the obligation, to buy or sell an underlying asset at a specific price (strike price) on or before a specific date (expiration date). Stock hedging is a strategy used to reduce the risk of a portfolio by offsetting the potential loss in one stock with a gain in another stock.

One way to use options for stock hedging is through the use of protective puts. A protective put is an option contract that gives the holder the right to sell a stock at a specific price (strike price) on or before a specific date (expiration date). This strategy can be used to protect against a potential decline in the price of a stock in a portfolio. For example, an investor who owns a stock that they believe may decrease in value can purchase a protective put option at a strike price below the current market price of the stock. If the stock does decrease in value, the investor can exercise the option and sell the stock at the higher strike price, limiting their losses.

Another way to use options for stock hedging is through the use of covered calls. A covered call is an option strategy in which an investor holds a long position in an asset and writes (sells) call options on that same asset in an attempt to generate additional income. This strategy can be used to generate income while also reducing the risk of a portfolio. For example, an investor who owns a stock that they believe may not increase in value can sell a call option at a strike price above the current market price of the stock. If the stock does not increase in value, the investor keeps the premium received from selling the call option, which can offset any potential loss in the value of the stock.

It is important to note that hedging strategies are not without their own set of risks and that investors should consult with a financial advisor before implementing any hedging strategy.

Investment Philosophies

There are several different investment philosophies that investors can use to guide their investment decisions. Some of the most common include:

Warren Buffet's Investment Philosophies

Soggy cigar butt

The "Soggy Cigar Butt" investment philosophy is a term that was used to describe Warren Buffett's investment strategy during the early days of his career. This strategy involves buying stocks that are trading at a discount to their intrinsic value, similar to buying a soggy cigar butt that still has a little bit of tobacco left in it after it has been smoked.

The idea behind this strategy is to find companies that are undervalued by the market and that have some sort of underlying value. This could be in the form of a strong brand, a valuable asset, or a solid business model. By buying these companies at a discount, an investor can potentially generate a significant return on their investment over time.

Buffett used this strategy in the early days of his career, before he met his business partner Charlie Munger. During this time, he focused on finding undervalued companies that had strong fundamentals, but that were overlooked by the market. He would then hold onto these stocks for the long-term, allowing the underlying value of the company to eventually be reflected in the stock price.

One of the key advantages of the soggy cigar butt strategy is that it allows investors to buy into companies at a discount, which can potentially lead to higher returns. However, it also requires a great deal of research and analysis to identify undervalued companies, and investors must have a long-term investment horizon to allow for the underlying value of the company to be reflected in the stock price.

As Buffet's career progressed he and Charlie Munger started to develop a more holistic approach to investing and expanded their investment criteria's. Nevertheless, the soggy cigar butt strategy played a key role in Buffett's early investment success and it's an interesting insight into how he approached investing in his early days.

Value Investment

The value investment philosophy is a long-term investment strategy that is championed by Warren Buffett, one of the most successful investors of all time. The strategy is based on the principle of buying undervalued companies with strong fundamentals and holding onto them for the long-term.

The value investment philosophy is rooted in the belief that the stock market is not always efficient, and that there are times when a company's stock is trading at a price that is lower than its true value. By identifying these undervalued companies, investors can potentially generate significant returns over time as the market eventually recognizes the true value of the company.

To identify undervalued companies, value investors typically focus on a company's financial metrics, such as its earnings, cash flow, and dividends. They also consider other factors such as the company's management, competitive position, and growth prospects. Once a company is identified as undervalued, the investor will usually hold onto the stock for the long-term, allowing the market to eventually recognize the true value of the company.

One of the key advantages of the value investment philosophy is that it allows investors to buy into companies at a discount, which can potentially lead to higher returns. Additionally, it can also provide a margin of safety, which is important during volatile market conditions.

Buffett's value investment philosophy is based on the principle of "buying right" and being patient. He looks for companies that have a long-term track record of success, strong management, and a clear path to growth. He also looks for companies that are trading at a discount to their intrinsic value, and that have a "moat" or sustainable competitive advantage. He is also a fan of investing in simple businesses that are easy to understand, and that have a wide economic moat.

Overall, the value investment philosophy is a long-term investment strategy that requires patience, research, and a thorough understanding of the companies in which one is investing. It's not a get-rich-quick scheme, but instead, it's a methodical and disciplined approach to investing that has proven to be successful over time.

Margin of Safety

One of the key concepts in value investing is the "margin of safety", which refers to the difference between the intrinsic value of a stock and its market price. The intrinsic value of a stock is the value that is calculated based on the underlying fundamentals of the company, such as its earnings, dividends, and growth prospects. The market price, on the other hand, is the price at which a stock is currently trading on the stock market.

The margin of safety is essentially the buffer between the intrinsic value of a stock and its market price. By only buying stocks that are trading at a significant discount to their intrinsic value, investors can reduce their risk of losing money if the market price falls below the intrinsic value. This is because the margin of safety provides a cushion that can help protect investors against market fluctuations and unexpected events that can cause the market price to fall.

The importance of having a margin of safety when investing in stocks cannot be overstated. By only buying stocks that are trading at a significant discount to their intrinsic value, investors can reduce their risk and increase their chances of earning a positive return on their investment. This is because if the market price falls below the intrinsic value, the margin of safety will help protect against losses, and if the market price rises above the intrinsic value, the investor will earn a higher return on their investment.

It's also important to note that determining the intrinsic value of a stock can be challenging, and different investors may arrive at different valuations for the same stock. However, by using a combination of fundamental analysis and valuation techniques, investors can make a more informed judgement about the intrinsic value of a stock and the size of the margin of safety.

In summary, the margin of safety is an important concept in value investing, which refers to the difference between the intrinsic value of a stock and its market price. By only buying stocks that are trading at a significant discount to their intrinsic value, investors can reduce their risk and increase their chances of earning a positive return on their investment. It's also important for investors to use a combination of fundamental analysis and valuation techniques to determine the intrinsic value of a stock and the size of the margin of safety.

Mr Market

The concept of "Mr. Market" is a metaphor for the stock market and its tendency to fluctuate in irrational ways. It was introduced by Benjamin Graham, the father of value investing, in his book "The Intelligent Investor". The metaphor of Mr. Market represents the stock market as a person who is willing to buy and sell stocks at different prices, depending on his mood. Some days, he is overly optimistic, and other days, he is overly pessimistic.

This metaphor is used to illustrate the idea that the stock market is often driven by emotions and speculation, rather than by fundamentals and value. The market may be irrational in the short-term, as investors may be driven by fear or greed, leading to overreaction to news or other events. This can cause prices to fluctuate wildly and can make it difficult for investors to make rational decisions.

The author suggests that investors should not pay attention to these short-term fluctuations of the market, but rather focus on the long-term value of the company. By focusing on the fundamentals of the company and its long-term potential, investors can make more informed decisions and avoid being swayed by the emotions and speculation that drive the market in the short-term.

The author also suggests that investors should not be swayed by the constant news and predictions of market experts and analysts, instead, they should focus on the long-term value of the company, and not let the noise of the market affect their decision making.

It is also important to note that even though it is important to focus on the long-term value of the company, it is not advisable to completely ignore the short-term market fluctuations. Investors should also keep an eye on the current market conditions and adjust their investment strategies accordingly.

In summary, the concept of "Mr. Market" serves as a reminder that the stock market can be irrational in the short-term, driven by emotions and speculation. The author suggests that investors should focus on the long-term value of the company and not pay attention to short-term market fluctuations, in order to make more informed decisions and avoid being swayed by emotions and speculation. Additionally, investors should also keep an eye on the current market conditions and adjust their investment strategies accordingly.

Other Investment Philosophies

Growth investing

This philosophy focuses on investing in companies that are growing rapidly, regardless of their current price. The goal is to buy companies that are expected to grow at a faster rate than the market average.

Momentum investing

This philosophy is based on the idea that stocks that have performed well in the past will continue to perform well in the future. The goal is to buy stocks that are trending upward, and to sell them when they start to decline.

Index investing

This philosophy is based on the idea that it is difficult to consistently beat the market, so investors should simply try to match the performance of the market. The goal is to buy a basket of stocks that represents the market as a whole, such as an index fund.

Contrarian investing

This philosophy is based on the idea that the market is often wrong and that by going against the crowd, investors can achieve higher returns. The goal is to buy stocks that are out of favor with the market, and to sell them when they become popular again.

Quantitative investing

This philosophy is based on the idea that by using complex mathematical models, investors can identify profitable investment opportunities that the market has overlooked. The goal is to use data and statistics to identify undervalued stocks.

Each investment philosophy has its own set of advantages and disadvantages, and investors should choose the one that best aligns with their investment goals and risk tolerance.

Chapter 10

Diversifying Portfolio with Alternative Investments

Debt vs Equity

Debt and equity are two primary types of financial instruments that companies use to raise capital. They represent two different ways in which investors can participate in the ownership of a company.

Debt instruments, such as bonds, are a way for companies to borrow money from investors. When an investor buys a bond, they are lending money to the company, and in return, the company agrees to pay interest on the loan and return the principal amount at maturity. Bonds are considered less risky than equity investments, as the company is obligated to repay the loan regardless of its performance.

On the other hand, equity instruments, such as stocks, represent a share of ownership in a company. When an investor buys a stock, they become a shareholder in the company and have a claim on its profits and assets. Equity investments are considered more risky than debt investments, as shareholders' returns are dependent on the company's performance.

In summary, debt represents a company's obligation to pay back borrowed money with interest, while equity represents a share of ownership in a company.

Investment in Debt Instruments

There are several different types of debt investments that an investor can make, each with its own set of pros and cons. Some of the most common types include:

Fixed deposits

Fixed deposits, also known as term deposits, are a type of debt investment where an investor loans money to a bank or financial institution for a fixed period of time, typically ranging from a few months to several years. In return, the bank or financial institution pays the investor a fixed rate of interest. In terms of tax implications, fixed deposits are generally considered to be tax-efficient investments. Interest earned on fixed deposits is subject to tax, but the rate of tax depends on the investor's income tax slab. For individuals and HUF, the interest income is added to the total income and taxed as per the income tax slab rate of the individual.

Debt mutual funds

Debt mutual funds are a type of investment vehicle that pools money from multiple investors to invest in a diversified portfolio of debt securities such as government bonds, corporate bonds, treasury bills, and other fixed-income securities. In terms of tax implications, debt mutual funds are considered to be relatively tax-efficient investments. The interest income earned on the debt securities held in the fund is subject to tax, but the rate of tax depends on the holding period of the fund. If the debt mutual fund is held for less than 36 months, the capital gains will be considered as short-term capital gains and taxed at the investor's marginal tax rate. If the debt mutual fund is held for more than 36 months, the capital gains will be considered as long-term capital gains and taxed at 20% with indexation benefit.

Treasury Bonds

These are bonds issued by the federal government and are considered to be among the safest debt investments available. They offer a fixed rate of interest and have a maturity of 30 years. They are considered as safe haven investments during times of economic uncertainty.

Corporate Bonds

These are bonds issued by corporations and offer higher interest rates than Treasury bonds. They are considered to be riskier than Treasury bonds, as the risk of default by the issuing company is higher.

Municipal Bonds

These are bonds issued by state and local governments and are often tax-exempt, making them an attractive option for investors in high tax brackets. They are considered to be less risky than corporate bonds and can offer a steady stream of income.

High-yield Bonds

Also known as "junk bonds," these are bonds issued by companies that are considered to be at a higher risk of default. They offer higher interest rates than other types of bonds but are considered to be much riskier investments.

Floating Rate Bonds

These bonds have a variable interest rate that adjusts based on market conditions. This type of bond is considered to be less risky than fixed rate bonds as the interest rate risk is less in floating rate bonds.

Each type of debt investment has its own set of pros and cons. Treasury bonds are considered to be the safest, but they also offer the lowest returns. Corporate bonds offer higher returns, but they also come with a higher risk of default. Municipal bonds are tax-exempt and are considered to be less risky than corporate bonds, but they can be affected by the financial health of the issuing municipality. High-yield bonds offer the highest returns, but they also come with a very high risk of default.

It is important to consider an investor's risk tolerance, investment horizon, and overall financial goals when choosing which type of debt investment to make. Diversifying the portfolio by investing in different types of debt instruments will also be a good strategy for an investor to manage the risk.

Types of Debt Mutual Funds

Debt mutual funds are a type of investment vehicle that invest primarily in fixed-income securities such as bonds and government securities. There are several different types of debt mutual funds, each with its own set of characteristics and risks.

Gilt Funds

These funds invest in government securities, which are considered to be among the safest investments available. Gilt funds are less risky than other types of debt funds but also offer lower returns.

Corporate Bond Funds

These funds invest in bonds issued by companies, which offer higher returns than government securities but also come with a higher level of risk. Corporate bond funds can be further divided into short-term and long-term funds.

Short-term Bond Funds

These funds invest in bonds that have a maturity of less than 3 years, and are considered to be less risky than long-term bond funds. They are suitable for investors who are looking for regular income and are not comfortable with taking higher risk.

Long-term Bond Funds

These funds invest in bonds that have a maturity of more than 3 years, and are considered to be more risky than short-term bond funds. They are suitable for investors who are looking for capital appreciation over a longer period of time.

Floating Rate Funds

These funds invest in bonds that have a floating interest rate, which can adjust to changes in market interest rates. They are considered less risky than bond funds that have fixed interest rates.

Hybrid Funds

These funds invest in a combination of debt and equity securities, providing a balance of income and growth opportunities.

Advantages of Debt Mutual Funds over FD/Bonds

There are several reasons why investing in debt mutual funds may be better than investing in fixed deposits (FDs) or bonds:

Diversification: Debt mutual funds invest in a diversified portfolio of debt securities, which helps to spread the risk across multiple investments. This diversification can help to reduce the overall risk of the portfolio.

Flexibility: Debt mutual funds offer more flexibility than fixed deposits or bonds. Investors can easily buy or sell units of the fund on a daily basis, whereas fixed deposits or bonds usually have a fixed maturity period.

Higher returns: Debt mutual funds have the potential to generate higher returns than fixed deposits or bonds. This is because the fund manager can actively manage the portfolio and switch between different debt securities to take advantage of changing market conditions.

Credit risk: Debt mutual funds are exposed to credit risk, which is the risk that the issuer of the debt security will default on its payments. However, mutual funds invest in a diversified portfolio of debt securities, which helps to spread the risk. On the other hand, when you invest in a bond, you are exposed to credit risk of the issuer alone.

Liquidity: Debt mutual funds are more liquid than bonds, as they can be easily bought and sold on the stock exchange. This means that investors can access their money more quickly and easily if they need to.

In summary, debt mutual funds offer diversification, flexibility, higher returns potential, and liquidity which make them a better option compared to fixed deposits or bonds. It is important to understand that, as with any investment, debt mutual funds come with their own set of risks and it's important to consult a financial advisor to understand which is the best option for you.

Risks Associated with Investment in Debt Instruments

Investing in debt financial instruments, such as bonds and fixed deposits, can provide a relatively low-risk opportunity for investors to earn a return on their investment. However, there are still risks associated with these types of investments.

Credit risk: One of the main risks associated with investing in debt financial instruments is credit risk. This refers to the risk that the issuer of the bond or fixed deposit will default on their debt obligations. This can happen if the issuer's financial condition deteriorates, or if they become unable to meet their debt repayment obligations. To mitigate this risk, investors can research the creditworthiness of the issuer before investing, and diversify their investments across different issuers.

Interest rate risk: Another risk associated with investing in debt financial instruments is interest rate risk. This refers to the risk that changes in interest rates will negatively impact the value of the bond or fixed deposit. When interest rates rise, the value of existing bonds and fixed deposits will typically decline, as they have a fixed interest rate. To mitigate this risk, investors can invest in bonds and fixed deposits with shorter maturities, or invest in floating rate debt securities that adjust to changes in interest rates.

Inflation risk: Inflation risk is the risk that the rate of inflation will outpace the rate of return on the investment. This can erode the purchasing power of the investor's returns and can be mitigated by investing in inflation-protected securities, such as Treasury Inflation-Protected Securities (TIPS).

Liquidity risk: Liquidity risk is the risk that an investment cannot be easily sold or converted into cash. This can be an issue with some debt securities, particularly those with longer maturities or lower credit ratings. To mitigate this risk, investors can focus on investing in more liquid debt securities, such as those traded on a stock exchange.

Overall, investing in debt financial instruments can provide a relatively low-risk opportunity for investors to earn a return on their investment, but it is important to be aware of the risks and to diversify investments. It's always recommended to consult with a financial advisor before making any investment decisions.

Alternative Investments

Gold

Gold is a popular investment choice due to its perceived stability and value. As an investment, gold can be bought in physical form, such as coins or bullion, or in the form of gold futures, options, or exchange-traded funds (ETFs).

Advantages of investing in gold include:

Hedge against inflation: Gold is considered a hedge against inflation as its value tends to increase when the purchasing power of the dollar decreases.

Diversification: Gold can be used to diversify an investment portfolio, as it tends to have low correlation with other assets such as stocks and bonds.

Liquidity: Gold is a liquid asset that can be easily bought and sold, providing investors with flexibility.

Store of value: Historically, gold has been used as a store of value and a medium of exchange. It has been used as a currency for thousands of years and is widely recognized as a valuable asset.

Disadvantages of investing in gold include:

Volatility: The price of gold can be volatile and subject to fluctuations, which can make it a risky investment.

Storage costs: Physical gold must be stored and insured, which can add to the cost of the investment.

Limited returns: Gold does not generate any income, and its returns are limited to price appreciation or depreciation.

Lack of cash flow: Gold does not generate any cash flow, unlike other investments like bonds which pay interest or dividends.

It's important to note that gold is not suitable for all investors, and the price of gold can be affected by many factors such as global economic conditions, interest rates, and geopolitical events. Before investing in gold, it's important to conduct proper research and due diligence, and to consider your risk tolerance and financial goals.

Commercial Real Estate

Commercial real estate refers to properties that are used for business purposes, such as office buildings, retail spaces, warehouses, and apartment buildings. Investing in commercial real estate can be a way to generate income through rental income and appreciation.

Advantages of investing in commercial real estate include:

Potential for high returns: Commercial real estate has the potential to generate higher returns than other types of investments, such as stocks or bonds.

Income generation: Commercial real estate can generate income through rental payments, which can provide a steady stream of cash flow.

Tax benefits: Commercial real estate can offer tax benefits, such as deductions for depreciation and interest expenses.

Appreciation: The value of commercial real estate can appreciate over time, providing potential for capital gains.

Hedge against inflation: Real estate generally tends to increase in value with inflation which acts as a hedge against inflation

Disadvantages of investing in commercial real estate include:

High initial investment: Investing in commercial real estate can require a significant amount of capital, which can be a barrier for some investors.

Risk of vacancy: The risk of vacancy is a major concern for commercial real estate investors, as a vacant property will not generate income.

Complexity: Investing in commercial real estate can be complex and time-consuming, involving various legal and financial considerations.

Maintenance costs: Commercial properties require regular maintenance, which can be costly and eat into profits.

Long-term commitment: Commercial real estate investments typically require a long-term commitment, which can limit an investor's flexibility.

It's important to note that commercial real estate investments can vary widely in terms of risk and return, and it's important to conduct proper research and due diligence before investing. It's also important to consider the location, condition and the quality of the property and the creditworthiness of the tenants before investing, and to consider your risk tolerance and financial goals.

Real estate investment trusts (RIET)

Real estate investment trusts (REITs) are companies that own, operate, or finance income-producing real estate. REITs provide investors with an opportunity to invest in a diversified portfolio of properties, such as office buildings, shopping centers, or apartment complexes, without the need to buy and manage individual properties.

Advantages of investing in REITs include:

Diversification: REITs can provide diversification for an investment portfolio, as they are not highly correlated with other asset classes such as stocks or bonds.

High yield: REITs tend to pay high dividends, which can provide a steady stream of income for investors.

Liquidity: REITs are traded on stock exchanges, which makes them easy to buy and sell.

Professional management: REITs are professionally managed, which means that the properties and the tenants are managed by experienced managers.

Access to real estate investment: REITs provide investors with access to real estate investment opportunities that would otherwise be difficult or impossible to access.

Disadvantages of investing in REITs include:

Volatility: REITs can be volatile and subject to fluctuations in the stock market, which can make them a risky investment.

Lack of control: Investors have little control over the management and operations of the properties, which can limit their ability to influence the performance of the investment.

Interest rate risk: REITs are sensitive to interest rate changes, as higher interest rates will increase the cost of borrowing for the REITs and can negatively affect the dividends.

Dividend cut risk: Dividends from REITs are not guaranteed, and the company may reduce or eliminate dividends in difficult times.

Management fees and expenses: REITs may charge management fees, which can reduce the return on investment.

It's important to note that REITs may perform differently from the overall stock market and from other types of real estate investments, and it's important to conduct proper research and due diligence before investing in REITs. It's also important to consider the type of properties, the location of the properties and the creditworthiness of the tenants before investing, and to consider your risk tolerance and financial goals.

Collectibles

Collectibles, such as art, coins, stamps, and sports memorabilia, can be a unique and exciting form of investment. However, they also come with their own set of advantages and disadvantages.

Advantages of investing in collectibles include:

Potential for appreciation: Some collectibles can appreciate in value over time, potentially providing a significant return on investment.

Emotional value: Collectibles can hold significant emotional value for the collector, making them a personal and meaningful investment.

Limited supply: Collectibles are often limited in supply, which can increase their value as demand increases.

Hedge against inflation: Collectibles can be a hedge against inflation, as their value may increase in line with inflation.

Tax benefits: Collectibles may offer certain tax benefits, such as the ability to take a capital loss on a collectible in the year it was sold.

Disadvantages of investing in collectibles include:

Illiquidity: Collectibles are often difficult to sell, as they require a specific buyer with an interest in that particular item.

High costs: Collectibles can be expensive to purchase, and also to store, insure and maintain.

Lack of transparency: The market for collectibles can be opaque, making it difficult to determine the true value of an item.

Lack of standardization: There is no standardized system of grading or certification for collectibles, which can make it difficult to evaluate the quality and value of an item.

Risk of fraud: Collectibles are a common target for fraud, and it can be difficult to verify the authenticity of an item.

It's important to note that collectibles are considered a speculative investment, and the historical performance of collectibles doesn't guarantee future performance. Before investing in collectibles, it's important to conduct thorough research, and to be prepared for the risks and costs associated with owning and maintaining them. It's also important to consider the potential tax implications and the fact that the value may fluctuate with market conditions.

Portfolio Allocation

Portfolio allocation is the process of dividing an investment portfolio among different asset classes, such as stocks, bonds, and cash, in order to achieve a specific investment goal. In personal financial planning, portfolio allocation is an important part of creating a well-diversified investment strategy that aligns with an individual's risk tolerance, investment time horizon, and financial goals.

When allocating assets to a portfolio, it's important to consider the trade-off between risk and return. Stocks generally have a higher potential for return, but also a higher level of risk. Bonds, on the other hand, tend to have a lower potential for return but also a lower level of risk. Cash and cash equivalents, such as savings accounts and money market funds, have the lowest potential for return but also the lowest level of risk.

A commonly used strategy for portfolio allocation is the "60-40" rule, which suggests allocating 60% of the portfolio to stocks and 40% to bonds. This provides a balance between higher-risk, higher-return investments and lower-risk, lower-return investments. However, the appropriate allocation will depend on an individual's risk tolerance, investment time horizon, and financial goals.

For example, if an individual has a long-term investment horizon, they may be able to tolerate a higher level of risk in their portfolio, and therefore allocate a greater percentage of their portfolio to stocks. On the other hand, if an individual is nearing retirement and needs to preserve their capital, they may want to allocate a greater percentage of their portfolio to bonds and cash to reduce the risk of losing their savings.

In addition to traditional asset classes, an individual's portfolio may also include alternative investments such as real estate, private equity, and hedge funds. These types of investments can provide diversification and the potential for higher returns, but they also come with higher levels of risk.

In conclusion, portfolio allocation is an important part of personal financial planning. It involves dividing an investment portfolio among different asset classes, such as stocks, bonds, and cash, in order to achieve a specific investment goal. The appropriate portfolio allocation will depend on an individual's risk tolerance, investment time horizon, and financial goals. A well-diversified portfolio that aligns with an individual's risk tolerance and investment goals can help them achieve their financial objectives over the long-term.

What Not to Do as a Long-Term Investor

Leverage/margin

Using leverage or margin to buy stocks can amplify returns, but it also amplifies the risks. A long-term investor should stay away from using leverage because it can be very risky.

For example, let's say an investor has $10,000 and wants to buy stock in XYZ company. Without leverage, they can only buy $10,000 worth of stock. However, if they use leverage, they can buy $20,000 worth of stock by borrowing $10,000.

If the stock price goes up, the investor will make a higher return on their investment because they have more shares. However, if the stock price goes down, the investor will lose more money because they have more shares. This is particularly true when the investor leverages their positions to the point that they become highly leveraged, meaning they have a high debt-to-equity ratio.

In addition, if the stock price drops significantly, the investor may be forced to sell their shares at a loss in order to meet margin calls. This can be detrimental to the long-term investor's portfolio and may cause them to miss out on any potential long-term recovery in the stock price.

Therefore, it is generally recommended for long-term investors to avoid using leverage when buying stocks and instead focus on investing in a diversified portfolio of stocks and bonds using their own capital. This will help them mitigate the risks associated with a single stock and allow them to stay invested for the long-term.

Intraday Trading

Intraday trading, also known as day trading, is a strategy where an investor buys and sells securities within the same trading day. It is a highly speculative and risky form of investing, and is not recommended for long-term investors.

One of the main reasons why long-term investors should stay away from intraday trading is because it is based on short-term market movements and can be affected by a wide range of unpredictable factors. For example, a piece of unexpected news or a sudden change in market sentiment can cause a stock to experience significant price fluctuations within a single day. This can result in large losses for the day trader, who may not have the time or knowledge to properly react to such events.

Another reason why long-term investors should avoid intraday trading is because it requires a significant amount of time and attention. Day traders need to constantly monitor the markets and make quick decisions based on short-term price movements. This can be incredibly stressful and time-consuming, and can take away from other important aspects of an individual's life.

Crypto

Cryptocurrency, such as Bitcoin, Ethereum, and Litecoin, is a digital or virtual currency that uses cryptography for security. It can be highly speculative and risky form of investing, and is not recommended for long-term investors.

One of the main reasons why long-term investors should stay away from cryptocurrency is because it is a highly speculative and volatile market. The value of a cryptocurrency can be affected by a wide range of factors, such as market sentiment, regulatory changes, and even hacking or fraud. These factors can cause significant price fluctuations, making it difficult for long-term investors to predict the future value of their investments.

Another reason why long-term investors should avoid cryptocurrency is because it is a relatively new and untested market. The technology behind cryptocurrencies is still evolving, and there is a lack of fundamental data and analysis to predict the long-term value of these assets. Additionally, the regulatory environment for cryptocurrencies is still uncertain, and this can introduce an additional layer of risk for investors.

Naked Option Trading

Naked option trading, also known as uncovered option trading, is a strategy where an investor sells or writes options contracts without holding the underlying securities. This can be a highly speculative and risky form of investing, and is not recommended for long-term investors.

One of the main reasons why long-term investors should stay away from naked option trading is because it involves taking on a significant amount of risk. When you sell or write options contracts, you are essentially betting that the underlying stock will not move in a certain direction. However, if the stock does move in that direction, you could be on the hook for significant losses. For example, if you sell a call option on a stock and the stock price goes up, you will be obligated to sell the stock at a lower price than the market, resulting in a loss.

Another reason why long-term investors should avoid naked option trading is because it requires a high level of expertise and knowledge of options trading. In order to be successful at naked option trading, you need to have a deep understanding of how options work, how to price them, and how to manage the risk. This is not something that most long-term investors will have the time or experience to master.

Futures Trading

Futures trading is a type of investment where an investor agrees to buy or sell an asset, such as a commodity or currency, at a specified price and date in the future. While futures trading can be a useful tool for hedging risk or speculating on market movements, it is not recommended for long-term investors.

One of the main reasons why long-term investors should stay away from futures trading is because it is a highly speculative and volatile market. The value of a future contract can be affected by a wide range of factors, such as changes in supply and demand, interest rates, and even weather patterns. These factors can cause significant price fluctuations, making it difficult for long-term investors to predict the future value of their investments.

Another reason why long-term investors should avoid futures trading is because it requires a significant amount of expertise and knowledge to navigate. Understanding how different futures contracts are affected by different market factors and how to trade accordingly can be a complex and difficult task, which many long-term investors may not have the time or expertise to master.

Currency Trading

Currency trading, also known as forex trading, is the buying and selling of different currencies in the foreign exchange market. It can be a highly speculative and risky form of investing, and is not recommended for long-term investors.

One of the main reasons why long-term investors should stay away from currency trading is because it is a highly speculative and volatile market. The value of a currency can be affected by a wide range of factors, such as interest rates, economic growth, political events, and even natural disasters. These factors can cause significant price fluctuations, making it difficult for long-term investors to predict the future value of their investments.

Another reason why long-term investors should avoid currency trading is because it requires a significant amount of expertise and knowledge to navigate. Understanding how different currencies are affected by different economic, political and other factors, and how to trade accordingly can be a complex and difficult task, which many long-term investors may not have the time or expertise to master.

Commodity Trading

Commodity markets are markets where raw or primary products are exchanged. These raw materials are traded in bulk on organized markets, in forms of futures contract. Commodity trading can be a highly speculative and risky form of investing, and is not recommended for long-term investors.

One of the main reasons why long-term investors should stay away from commodity markets is because they are highly volatile and subject to a wide range of unpredictable factors. Commodities such as gold, oil, and agricultural products are affected by factors such as weather, geopolitical events, and even natural disasters. These events can cause significant price fluctuations, making it difficult for long-term investors to predict the future value of their investments.

Another reason why long-term investors should avoid commodity markets is because they require a significant amount of expertise and knowledge to navigate. Commodities are not just affected by their own specific factors but also by the broader economy, interest rates, and currency fluctuations. Understanding how these factors affect commodity prices and how to trade accordingly can be a complex and difficult task, which many long-term investors may not have the time or expertise to master.

Conclusion

In conclusion, developing a mindset for financial freedom is crucial for achieving long-term financial security and wealth creation. By understanding financial literacy and the role of emotions in decision making, we can make better financial decisions and avoid common pitfalls. Additionally, understanding key financial concepts such as assets and liabilities, active and passive income, and the power of compounding can help us grow our wealth over time.

One of the key takeaways from this book is the importance of financial planning and budgeting, as well as shifting from a saving mindset to an investing mindset. By developing financial discipline and following a step-by-step process for getting rich, we can work towards achieving our financial goals.

The story of Warren Buffet serves as a powerful reminder of the potential of long-term disciplined investing, diversification, and risk management. By focusing on these principles, we can increase our chances of success in the world of investing.

In addition, achieving financial freedom is a journey that requires a solid understanding of the math behind accumulating wealth, as well as a clear plan for building and diversifying your portfolio. We've covered key concepts such as future and present value, recurring payments, and the difference between active and passive income. We've also discussed strategies for investing in the stock market, including understanding equity and the different types of equity investments. Additionally, we've covered alternative investments such as debt instruments, gold, commercial real estate, and collectibles.

One of the most important takeaways from this book is the importance of diversifying your portfolio. Diversification helps to spread risk and can lead to better returns over the long term. We also emphasized the importance of avoiding common mistakes, such as leverage and intraday trading, that can lead to financial ruin.

As you continue on your journey towards financial freedom, remember to stay focused on your long-term goals, and to always do your own research and due diligence before making any investment decisions. With persistence and discipline, you can achieve the financial freedom that you desire.

Remember, achieving financial freedom is not just about having a lot of money, it's about having the freedom to live the life you want to live. Whether it's traveling, starting a business, or just enjoying life with your family, financial freedom gives you the ability to make those choices.

We hope that this book has provided you with valuable insights and strategies to help you on your journey towards financial freedom. As you implement what you've learned in this book, we wish you all the best in your efforts to build wealth and achieve your financial goals.

About The Author

Shubham has a diverse background, which he applies to his role as an author. He is a software developer, and has made notable achievements in the technology industry.

Shubham holds an engineering degree in Computer Science and Technology, and has put his education to good use throughout his career. He has worked as a software developer for some of the biggest names in the tech industry, including "Big 4" MNCs. In this role, he has gained valuable experience in the development and implementation of cutting-edge technologies, as well as a deep understanding of the industry as a whole.

In addition to his professional work in technology, Shubham is also a passionate personal finance expert and investor. His interests lie in the areas of personal finance, investment and philosophy, and he finds inspiration in the teachings of one of the greatest investors of all time, Warren Buffet. He has spent many years studying and researching these topics, and is well-versed in the strategies and principles that can help individuals achieve financial success.

When he is not working or studying, Shubham can be found indulging in his hobbies, which include exercising, playing cricket, table tennis, and taking road trips. These activities not only provide him with the opportunity to relax and unwind, but also help him stay physically and mentally fit.

Shubham is a dedicated and hardworking individual who is committed to sharing his knowledge and experience with others. For this He manages a community called "Engineering Wealth" for people having similar mindset

Engineering Wealth

"Engineering Wealth" is a community of people sharing wealth-creating mindset. Our mission is to empower individuals to take control of their financial future by combining a growth mindset with actionable strategies. We strongly believe that having the community of people sharing similar mindset would help us all achieve success in a much better way. This platform is dedicated to promoting the ideas of "Money Mindset and Math: Unlocking Financial Freedom through Mindset and Action.

Our team consists of experienced professionals and financial experts who are dedicated to providing valuable insights and practical advice on how to achieve financial freedom.

Through our community, you will find a wealth of information on personal Finance and Investments. Join us on our mission to unlock financial freedom and start engineering your wealth today.

Join the Community Now

website: https://www.engineeringwealth.in

Instagram: (@engineering_wealth_)

https://www.instagram.com/engineering_wealth_/

Facebook: (@joinengineeringwealth)

https://www.facebook.com/joinengineeringwealth/

LinkedIn:

https://www.linkedin.com/in/shubhamsxn/

Email:

joinengineeringwealth@gmail.com

Review Ask

Thank you for taking the time to read our Book. We hope you have found the content informative and helpful.

We are constantly looking for ways to improve and provide valuable information to our readers. We would greatly appreciate your feedback on the content of our book.

Your review and comments will help us understand what you liked or didn't like about the book, and give us insights on how we can make it better. We also value your feedback on how we can make the book more accessible and engaging for you.

We would be honored if you could spare a few minutes to leave a review of our book on **Amazon**, **Goodreads**, or any other book review platform that you prefer.

Your feedback is essential to our ongoing efforts to create high-quality content that is relevant, informative and enjoyable to read.

Thank you for your support, and we hope you continue to enjoy our work in the future.

Best regards,

Shubham Saxena

 **Scan this QR code to write a review on Amazon**

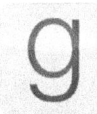 **Scan this QR code to write a review on Goodreads**

www.ingramcontent.com/pod-product-compliance
Lightning Source LLC
Chambersburg PA
CBHW052350220526
45465CB00003BA/1040